THE
FAMILY–
BUSINESS
BALANCING
ACT

THE
FAMILY–
BUSINESS
BALANCING
ACT

AN ENTREPRENEUR'S GUIDE
TO BEING A FAMILY MAN

PATRICK CUMMINGS

LIONCREST

THE FAMILY—BUSINESS BALANCING ACT
An Entrepreneur's Guide to Being a Family Man

ISBN   978-1-5445-3236-3   *Hardcover*

978-1-5445-3237-0   *Paperback*

978-1-5445-3238-7   *Ebook*

CONTENTS

To my most important clients,
my family: Brooke, Bryce, and Morgan.

You mean the world to me!

INTRODUCTION

MY DAD GREW UP IN A LOGGING FAMILY. HIS OWN FATHER worked hard, long hours at the mill and in the woods six days a week. When he came home, he expected the cooking, cleaning, and parenting to be done. His role, as he saw it, was largely that traditional place reserved for fathers: the breadwinner. And that was it.

I think my dad wanted to be a better father to his children. He certainly didn't want us to grow up as a logging family with logging our likely only possible future career. He wanted to start us on a new path. And he succeeded on that front. Instead of working in the mill, he earned a track scholarship at Eastern Washington University, got a degree in physical education, and went on to be a high school coach. His hard work definitely opened new doors for his sons.

That success, though, came at a price. My dad loved his job, but it threw the rest of his life out of balance. Back then, a coach at a small high school coached every sport. There wasn't much time left over for anything else. He had even less time after he took a position as an athletic director. At that point, he began hosting state track and district basketball tournaments—adding a full-time job on top of his full-time duties as an athletic director.

This left very little room for him to do the parenting he meant to do. My experience as his son proves it. Almost all of my childhood memories with my father revolve around his work. My earliest memory of my father is watching one of his teams win the state championship. Most of my memories of the weekends I spent at his house include helping him complete some task for his job, like filling out basketball brackets instead of spending time with his kids. Our "quality" time together often amounted to prepping the gymnasium for a tournament or repairing the track.

He simply had very few resources left to participate in the activities that my brother and I loved—and little chance for him to develop the deep, loving relationships with us that I think he wanted. From an early age, I enjoyed hunting and fishing, but because my father had to host Friday night football games every week in the fall, it was a rare Saturday he could get up early enough to go out into nature with us.

When I look back on my childhood reflections of my father, the sad thing is, all I see is a man working far too much—a man who wanted to be a good family man but who just didn't have the time, energy, or ability to actually focus on his family.

WHAT DO YOUR KIDS THINK OF YOUR PRIORITIES?

For all his faults, my father was not a bad man. He loved his sons, and I am confident that he wanted to achieve a balance between his ambitions at work and his role as a dad. Football games made it difficult to go hunting early on a Saturday morning, but he did do it when he could. After my parents divorced, he welcomed my brother to move in with him. He avoided disciplining me on the weekends I spent with him not because he didn't care but because he was afraid that I wouldn't want to visit him otherwise.

As he got older and finally had time away from work, it hurt him deeply that he wasn't close to his sons. He told me later on that it was the biggest regret of his life.

His problem wasn't a lack of love or desire to be a good parent; it was the fact he didn't know how to do it. He didn't know how to balance his work with his family obligations. He didn't know how to communicate his love effectively. He didn't know how to share experiences or nurture interests in his children. He didn't know how to strike the balance between discipline and love—either being too strict with my brother or too lenient on me.

With the benefit of decades of fatherhood, I can see all that now, but as a child it was mystifying and hurtful. As a boy, it seemed to me that Dad always put work first and family second. All I saw was a man who didn't know how to connect to me. I longed for my father's attention, but I grew up accepting that I couldn't have it.

How much of my father's story matches your own experience as a son—and your fears about your role as a father? Did your father work too much? Do you work such long hours you miss most of the parenting you wanted to be doing? Did Dad always come home grouchy? Do you bring stress home and sometimes snap at your family? Was your father the silent type? Do you struggle to communicate how you feel or why you aren't more available? Was Dad the disciplinarian? Do you regularly miss the mark on discipline either as the grumpy taskmaster always quick to punish or the friend who lets the kids get away with murder?

These mistakes are all very understandable. Fathers have traditionally been expected to work as much as possible in order to provide for their families. For a long time, that was the sole qualification for good fathering. Even now, men are usually expected to prioritize work over everything else in their lives. And you have likely done so throughout your own career. You are, after all, an entrepreneur, and therefore already have significant demands placed on your time, energy, and attention. You have a business to build and to run. You have responsibilities not just to your family but to employees and customers—and possibly investors. It's a lot to juggle. No wonder you regularly drop the ball.

And yet, when you take a step back, you have to ask yourself, how do you think your kids see you now? Do they see the impressive, hard-working entrepreneur you want them to see, or do they see a dad who is never there to tuck them in or make them breakfast—a dad who is always too tired and distracted to really be their father?

If it is the latter, you have to further ask yourself this: Are you willing to accept the consequences for the lack of family-business balance in your life? And if that sounds like a bad trade, are you ready to do what it takes to change those dynamics and to be the family man you intended to be?

YOUR WORK IS ACTUALLY A BLESSING

When looking over your responsibilities as an entrepreneur, it's easy to see limitations instead of opportunity in regard to your role as a parent. You may not want to be a father who misses all the big moments in your children's lives or who fails to create those strong ties that will hold throughout life, but what can you do? Entrepreneurs are famous for their long hours and the exhausting list of duties. That's what it takes to make a business a success. And it's also what it takes to be a successful parent. How can you find balance in both worlds when you only have so many hours and so much energy?

But entrepreneurship is far more of a blessing than it may seem to you at first—because through your role as a business owner you have more freedom to make better choices in your work and your family life. Most people work in an office and have very little control over their schedules and priorities. They can't always take a Tuesday off for a sick kid or leave early on Fridays to watch their kid play tennis. You have that flexibility. It isn't easy to take advantage of it, but it is available. And that means you have the potential to be a good family man and a good businessman—so long as you learn how to balance all those responsibilities.

I've personally lived the difference owning a business makes. Before I ran my own company, I worked for a big corporation out of Switzerland. In exchange for a good salary, I was moved around like a pawn piece on a chessboard. My first assignment was in Pierre, South Dakota, where I was told I would spend at least six months. Six weeks later, the company moved me to Sioux City, Iowa. I had no say over my location or my time, and because of that, I hardly ever saw my family. If I'd asked for a position back in Washington so I could at least wake up and say goodnight to my kids, my boss would have told me to find a job at another company.

Not only was my schedule impossible, I was also under immense financial pressure that I had no ability to relieve. If I had a good year, I was told to meet or beat those numbers next year—or else live without a bonus. Territories were always getting bigger; sales were expected to grow at every opportunity.

Essentially, I was expected to put work before family every single day of the year—for the rest of my career.

So while your responsibilities as an entrepreneur are undeniably significant, it's important to recognize that you are lucky. You are lucky to have a family you love and that you want to spend more time with. And you are lucky to be in a position to create a balance between your work and that family. You are your own boss, and that means you can accommodate your own life. No one is above you demanding you work more hours over the weekend or get into the office before dawn.

The reason you haven't made the necessary changes to create that balance is because, like most entrepreneurs, you're probably the hardest boss you've ever had. You want your company to succeed. You want to provide a better life for your kids and your spouse. And that motivation can make it hard to justify a day off or an early exit from the office.

If you can open yourself to a different approach to entrepreneurship and fatherhood, though, it's possible to make all of this work. You can be a success in the office, be a supportive, loving partner to your spouse, and be a great dad that your kids look up to for the rest of their lives. You can fit it all in. And this book is going to show you how to do it.

We're going to start by looking at how common this problem is for entrepreneurial fathers and how hard it is to overcome. We'll see how few resources and examples men have in the parenthood department, even as society—and our kids—have come to expect more from us. Then we'll look at how important it is that, despite these limitations, we get this part of our lives right. Our kids need us to be good fathers. Our spouses need us to be good husbands. It's no exaggeration to say that these will be the most consequential choices you make in your life.

To start making better choices, we'll focus on finding your deepest motivations so you know precisely what matters most in your life. Then we'll look at how you can transform that motivation into more time with your family by placing more value on that time, changing your office culture, and adjusting your schedule so that there's more room for the most important people in your life.

With your time better organized, we'll see how you can separate your work and home stress so you're in a better place mentally to be a father and an entrepreneur. Finally, we'll look at how you can build the strong relationships you want with your spouse and your kids through connecting to their interests, partnering in discipline, and communicating love—all while learning from the mistakes you will inevitably make along the way.

FOLLOW MY LEAD

I know that this process works because it worked for me. When my son, Bryce, was young, I made many of the same mistakes my father did. Like him, I wasn't home enough. Like him, when I was home, I was bringing stress into the household. And like him, I was watching my marriage disintegrate.

I turned it all around, all while building a very successful practice in my industry. I wasn't perfect. I still made plenty of mistakes. But I found a way to balance it all and be the best dad and best entrepreneur I could be. And because of that effort, my wife, Brooke, and I are still together and still parenting successfully. Bryce and my daughter, Morgan, are now happy, well-adjusted young adults—and they actually *like* spending time with me.

I've structured my work and my life so well that I'm now able to take ten weeks off a year and enjoy time doing what I love and spending it with the people I love.

THERE IS NO MAGIC BULLET

To be clear, getting to this point wasn't easy for me, and it won't be easy for you. Along the way, you'll encounter tough financial choices, conflicts with family and scheduling conflicts with the office, and a lot of people pushing you to make different choices—you'll meet some of those "guys" in the chapters ahead.

So if you've come here looking for easy answers, you're in the wrong place. The advice ahead is going to require a lot of work on your part. Running a business is hard, and so is being a father and a husband.

Good thing you're a hard worker.

If you're willing to put the effort in, this book is going to help you avoid the mistakes my dad made and that I almost made after him. It's going to help break that chain of fatherhood choices that leave men absent from their children's lives and leave their relationships with their children broken.

In my opinion, that's the most important work you can do. And I'm going to help you do it.

PART I

DAD CHALLENGES

CHAPTER 1

DEVELOPING A NEW TRADITION

MY PARENTS DIVORCED WHEN I WAS AROUND SIX. THE parents of my wife, Brooke, divorced when she was a teenager. Entering our marriage, all we knew was dysfunction. We knew how marriages failed. We knew how easily they could break apart. But we didn't know anything about how to make them succeed.

For many years, this never seemed like a setback. Early on, our marriage was strong and thriving. It's not very surprising, though, that after our children were born and work became more demanding, we came very close to walking away from our union the same way our parents had.

I don't want to undersell how intense the pressures we were facing were. At the time, Brooke was working weekends at a veterinary clinic that was forty-five minutes away. Because she had to be on call the entire time, she had to leave our house Friday night or Saturday morning and wouldn't be home until Monday. My schedule was the opposite, with long days throughout the workweek spent building my business.

The tension of navigating such conflicting schedules was inevitable, but worse than that tension was the distance. We hardly saw each other, and we were growing apart. We didn't really fight in that period—there were no intense shouting matches or thrown chairs like I'd seen from my parents—but that's because we weren't communicating at all. The closest we came to connecting was walking past each other in the hallway. There were no hugs and kisses, no warm words, no shared experiences. We were strangers living together who also happened to share two children.

Things went on this way for a couple years. At some point, we were either going to have to take some serious steps to repair our relationship or we were going to have to start considering a permanent separation.

One Saturday, we were finally confronted with the momentous choice in front of us. Brooke was about to head out for the weekend, and I realized that I was glad she was leaving. The kids were glad she was leaving because that meant less tension in the house. And I think Brooke was glad to be going as well. The family was splitting apart. I think we could all feel that the marriage had come to the breaking point. As she walked out the door, I fully expected that the next time I saw her, she'd be telling me that she didn't want to do this anymore.

When she came back on Monday, though, the discussion we had was very different from the one I had been rehearsing in mind all weekend. Instead of saying it was over, she told me she had contacted our pastor and asked for his help. She wanted us to work on fixing our marriage and keeping the family together.

To understand how hard it was for Brooke to take the lead like that, you have to understand that my wife is a serious introvert. She is never the one to go out of her way for a conversation, particularly a difficult one. Yet somehow, she found it in her to reach out to our pastor for guidance and to tell me how much she wanted to fix our relationship. Instead of preparing for the worst as I had done, she had managed to have an honest and forthright call with our pastor and take that first, huge step toward getting our family back on track.

It's no exaggeration to say that her effort on that weekend saved our marriage. If Brooke hadn't made that call, we wouldn't have made it. We were falling unwillingly into the habits we'd learned from our own parents. To break with the tradition we'd both be raised with, we'd both have to commit to stepping out of comfort zones. We'd have to make a conscious and dedicated effort to do better.

It was not an easy path to take, but it paid off. We're still together today.

FALLING INTO OLD HABITS

Perhaps the hardest part of being a good dad is that most of us struggle to find the resources to be the fathers we intend to be. That starts with a lack of good examples in our lives. Society has changed a lot in the last couple generations. In that time, we've seen families come to not just accommodate but expect two incomes instead of one. Gone are the days when fathers were the sole breadwinner whose only role in the household was relaxing in the recliner. These days, a man has to go to work and then come home to be a partner in household work and every aspect of parenting. Dads are supposed to work and go to school events—or stay home when the kid is sick, just like Mom.

These are all, to my mind, positive changes. It's great that fathers are expected to do more. The problem is that many of us didn't grow up with a father who showed us how to balance all these expectations. Over those same generations of transition, men have struggled to keep up with the changes. Some have found it difficult to support their spouse in the workplace or to do their share of the work at home. Men continue to be overworked, less present, and less active in the family than they mean to be. And unfortunately, far too often, fathers give up. They walk away through divorce, they become as detached as their fathers were.

Without a good example of modern fatherhood to draw from, it's hard for fathers—particularly those with significant work obligations like entrepreneurs—to know when they're doing enough. This can lead to all kinds of miscues, misunderstandings, and miscalculations. When things get tough and pressures mount, many men continue to default to the old standards they grew up with, prioritizing work and income over time with their spouse or their children. They show love through working themselves to the bone, never realizing they are leaving their children as unfulfilled as they felt when they were young.

THERE AREN'T ENOUGH GOOD FATHER AWARDS

Despite a general societal shift in expectations for men, we aren't helped along much by any corresponding shift in accommodation to meet those expectations. Society continues to *say* that men should prioritize family and work equally, all while sending constant signals that men should put work above all else.

When's the last time you heard someone praise a man for working less and taking care of the kids more? How often do you hear about the need for paternity leave so fathers have time to bond with their children? How many men are seen as fathers first and workers second? How many awards do we give to men for their parenting compared to the infinite awards we offer for success in business?

We live in a world in which Father's Day is still far less significant than Mother's Day, and in which a father is still expected to work longer hours and spend more time away from the family than his spouse.

This is all changing, but that change is coming more slowly than the expectations that have been set. It can create a real disconnect when fathers try to balance their obligations and priorities. On the one hand, they're praised for hard work far more than teaching their daughter to ride a bike. On the other hand, putting that work before the bike ride leads to criticism. It can feel like a no-win situation.

WE DON'T COMMUNICATE ENOUGH

Much of this tension could be eased through better communication, but communication can also be a struggle for men. Far too often, men don't communicate how they are feeling or what they are experiencing to their families. They don't relate the difficulties they feel in achieving balance to their spouses, which makes misunderstanding easier and compromise harder. They don't talk to their children about how hard they're trying to meet their children's needs, so their children are left to make assumptions about why Dad isn't home or why Dad is always grouchy when they ask to play with him.

We don't discuss what life will look like for the family if everyone wants Dad to be home more or if everyone feels the family needs more income. We simply make decisions and expect the family to live with them.

At the same time, men don't communicate enough with each other. We don't have enough fathers' groups where men can speak about their frustrations and find solutions together. We don't talk to our friends about the issues we're having or the stress we're under. And there aren't enough books written by men for fathers to help in making some of the transitions they need to make.

This leaves us in a very difficult situation. Times have changed, and we are ill-equipped for that change because we don't have enough good examples to draw from or support from society in general. And we make this harder on ourselves because we don't talk about it. We don't talk to our spouse or our kids. We don't talk to our friends. And we don't write or read books about this.

So how are we ever going to learn how to get that family-business balance right?

YOU WANT TO GET THIS RIGHT

The answer is we have to start this conversation. Fatherhood is simply too important to keep ignoring these struggles and trying to muddle our way through. As I told Brooke after we committed to fixing our family, "I'm committed. I'm not leaving—because I can't put our family through what either of us went through as children."

To repair our relationship and to become a better father, it took a lot of work. We went to a couples counseling group for six years. We had to learn how to communicate and how to handle the stress we were both under. But we put the work in because we knew how important this was.

That was the one blessing that came from being children of divorce: we knew how painful it was for a father to fall short of what a child needs from them. A father is incredibly important to a child's growth and development. Even if you don't win awards for it, being a good dad can make all the difference in your child's life. And if you get this wrong, it will have consequences: for you, your spouse, and your children.

CHAPTER 2

FAMILY MATTERS

I MET ABC CREDENTIALS GUY AT A CONFERENCE FOR entrepreneurs. I gave him that nickname because he lists every credential known to man after his real name. He's a tax attorney, and he's finished every course and every training available in his profession. He's received every award and bonus in the business. You could write a novel using his various titles.

We struck up a quick friendship, and after trading a few basic facts about our businesses, we started discussing family. It turned out, ABC Credentials Guy had inherited his drive for business success from his father. His dad had been a workaholic, and ABC Credentials Guy had followed in those same footsteps. Eventually, he'd even taken over his old man's business.

He wasn't a greedy man or materialistic—in fact he was extremely giving—but as I talked to him, I noticed that he clearly tied his entire sense of self-worth to whether he could outwork everyone else. He had to sign the best clients, offer the most impressive service, and get the biggest payouts. He bragged to me about how many extra workdays he could fit into a calendar year just by eking out an extra hour or two in the office each day.

"First in and last out, every day, always" was his motto.

He even worked on family vacations. He was never more than a few feet from a device that would allow him to respond to an email or a call. Nothing was more important than keeping his current clients happy and getting that next client to sign on to his firm.

In the years since we met, we've kept in touch at quarterly workshops, and I can say with absolute honesty that ABC Credential Guy is one of the smartest and most decent individuals I've ever met. He makes more money than most of us can imagine, and he gives most of it away. With the money he has leftover, he sends his kids to nice schools. He bought his family a very nice house, but I've never seen him spend much of anything on himself. Overall, he's a very admirable man.

But nice schools, a nice house, and being an overall upstanding guy wasn't enough for his family. Over the years, those long hours and the intense dedication to his business took a toll. Years of extra hours in the office, missing meals six days a week, and never turning work off left his family feeling dismissed and distant.

I heard from him again recently. On the Zoom call, I could see that he looked worn out and dispirited. When I asked what was going on, he mentioned a fight he'd had with his wife. In the midst of the argument, she asked him what he thought about getting a divorce.

"I couldn't believe it," he told me. "'Why are you talking about divorce,' I asked her, 'when I've provided so much for our family?'"

He shook his head. "She told me that it wasn't enough. What am I supposed to do now?"

He was mystified how it had come to this. He was not a hateful or cruel husband or father. He was kind and decent to everyone, especially his family. Yet because his roles as a spouse and a father always came after his work, he had begun to see himself on the outside of his family. And there were no credentials that could let him back in.

FATHERS ARE IMPORTANT

I don't remember ever having breakfast at home with my dad. We ate out at diners from time to time, but regular old boring breakfast with Dad never happened. And though that seems a small thing to worry about squeezing into a hectic family life, I know I missed out on something important.

I know that because much of my childhood was spent seeking father figures to fill in for the strong male presence that was too busy to share those little moments in my life. At the age of eight, I found a father figure in the form of an odd high school student who was a neighbor of ours. He was not a great influence. He didn't have a job, which was very rare in those days, and his behavior was beyond questionable. I remember witnessing him trying to sneak a peek at a girl who was changing. Once, he went street racing against someone from the next town over while I was in the backseat, all in an effort to impress some girls.

This teenager wasn't my last questionable male role model. In high school, there was a man who befriended me who would bring me alcohol. These events were only possible because my parents were too distracted to notice the sort of people I was interacting with. Dad was always coaching.

Mom was in grad school. And that meant I was at the mercy of any older figure who took an interest in me.

Unbelievably, I was one of the lucky ones. Living without a positive father figure can lead to far more serious consequences for children. If a little girl doesn't have a father figure in her life, she is likely to subconsciously search for that father figure in the form of older men. This is not guesswork. According to data collected by the US Census Bureau in 2020, that young woman is more likely to engage in sexual relationships, and she's seven times more likely to become pregnant as a teenager.

According to the same data, a little boy who grows up without a father figure is more likely to become violent in the home or commit crime. In general, a child, regardless of their sex, is far more likely to become impoverished, abuse drugs and alcohol, drop out of high school, and end up in prison.

This is the power you hold as a father. Without your love, your time, and your attention, your child can grow up seeking men who will give them the acceptance and sense of importance they need. If you aren't there, you can't control who these men are or what influence they have on your child. Without you, your child can grow up feeling unlovable and deserving of unhappiness or punishment for what they feel is some internal brokenness or failing.

These are not exaggerations. This is a well-documented phenomenon. And the sad stories behind these statistics are only going to get worse. Modern technology has made it so easy for children to reach out to these negative influences online. Through social media, a child can come to dwell on their sense that they have no value, and they can easily be preyed upon by those who lurk in the shadows.

It's your job to protect them from all of this. And I would argue, no matter what business you run, it's your most important job.

ENDING NEGATIVE CYCLES

The power of your role as a father goes even further. As a father, you create the template for what your children come to expect from themselves, their relationships, and the men who enter their lives.

Brooke and I came so close to divorce partly because we both grew up without examples of men who knew how to invest themselves in their families. Instead of learning how to argue and make up or how to forgive and strengthen a relationship, we'd learned that when things get tough, walk away. Moving away from that template proved extremely difficult.

Likewise, ABC Credentials Guy's struggles with balancing work and family came from observing a father who never tried to get that balance right. Work was all that mattered to his father, and ABC Credential Guy learned that lesson all too well.

So, you have to ask yourself, what template do you want to set for your children? You have the opportunity to be an example for them of a man who follows his dreams *and* takes care of his family. Your sons can grow up knowing that such balance is important and possible. Your daughters will know to expect that same balance from any men they grow close to. In fact, all your children can grow up knowing they should seek out men who work hard and provide care for others.

By showing affection to your spouse in front of your kids and giving that affection to them directly, you can show them how to express love and affection later in their own lives. By demonstrating how to overcome a disagreement with your partner in parenting, you can help them overcome arguments with their own future friends and romantic partners.

These are all positive cycles you can help create that are likely to help your children become happier and more fulfilled adults. But to create them, you have to be present, and your family has to be a priority.

TIME IS OF THE ESSENCE

I'm sure you agree with that final point. You wouldn't be reading this book if you didn't think being a good father was a priority. The only problem is you're extremely busy right now. Family is important, you might be saying, but business has to come first at the moment. You'll be a better dad later.

Before you put this book down for a few years with a promise to return when work stress eases up, you should recognize that you don't have as much "later" as you might think.

Your children yearn for your attention when they are young, and in those early years, they will soak up your influence. Your spouse needs your assistance in raising them and your affection to pull through these crucial, difficult years of parenting. But these circumstances will not always be true.

You only really have the ability to influence a child's decision-making up until they're twelve to fourteen years old.

At that point, nature has built-in a switch that goes off in their brains, and once it's flipped, they become far more suspicious of your influence and far less interested in your attention. This is true whether you're a great father or not—but it's particularly true if you have failed to dedicate that focus to them earlier in life.

If you haven't built a loving and respectful relationship by the time they hit puberty, it will be extremely difficult to do so after that switch flips. That doesn't mean it is impossible, but it is far harder to do with older, more independent children.

This was a tough lesson to learn for my father. As my brother, Scott, and I grew older, my dad became extremely regretful about how he behaved as a father, and he apologized to Scott when my brother was in his forties. By then, though, it simply wasn't enough. It would have taken far more to repair that relationship. And unfortunately for both of them—and for me—my father didn't have that much time left. He died before he could undo that damage and regain that connection.

Thinking of your children in their forties may feel like a lifetime from now, but trust me when I tell you that the years when you can immediately slip into their lives will pass far more quickly than you think. And once you miss that period, you have much less say over who they become and how much time they spend with you—whether they're sixteen, twenty-five, or forty-nine.

This is equally true of your relationship with your spouse. Your partner also isn't going to hang around forever if you don't ever prioritize that relationship. And that relationship may be unfixable once it truly breaks. They are not going to appreciate raising your kids largely on their own and pursuing their career with far less assistance from you. After the kids leave and there's no intimacy left in the household, how long will your spouse spend in that lonely home before seeking someone with more time for them?

Statistically, the most common times for divorce are after the second child is born—when time, energy, and patience are at their lowest point—when the kids are in their teens, and when they leave the house. My wife and I almost fell in that first hole, and if I had kept my focus exclusively on my business, I expect we wouldn't have even made it to the second or third.

I had to make that change early and commit to it. And so do you. If you want to be a better family man, you have to start making changes now. There's less time ahead to correct your choices than you think.

CREDENTIAL YOUR PARENTHOOD

During our conversation, ABC Credentials Guy eventually turned to the lack of appreciation his family had for him. In the midst of laying out his grievances, he began to list all the credentials he had worked on as an example of all he'd done for his family.

I pulled him up short.

"What credentials do you have for your role as a father and spouse?"

He gave me a confused look. "None. They don't give those out for family life."

"But if they did," I asked. "Which ones would you have earned? Would you have a credential for weekends spent with the kids? Or one for giving your wife time off for her interests? Would you have one for teaching your son to fish or one for taking your wife out once a month every month for a year? What have you done for your family that would deserve a letter after your name?"

The truth, he slowly realized, is that he wouldn't deserve any such award. He'd become a master of his business, but he'd failed to put that extra effort into being a father or a husband. This is often the case for entrepreneurs. In a vacuum, we will try to catch every fish in a lake. But this isn't a vacuum. It's a life filled with responsibilities to work *and* family. At some point, you have to make choices and set priorities. You can't have every fish, so you have to decide which fish are most important to you and how many you need.

That doesn't mean you have to abandon your company or give up on your dreams. But it does mean you've got to start making some decisions about how you want to spend your time and your energy—so you can make sure you always have enough for the most important people in your life.

PART II

MAKING TIME
FOR WHAT
MATTERS

CHAPTER 3

TAKING YOURSELF OFF DEFAULT

I LEFT THE CORPORATE WORLD IN 1999 RIGHT AFTER MY daughter, Morgan, was born. Her birth really clarified things for me. I had been sick of spending all my time on the road for a long time, but I realized that it was now imperative that I create a position for myself that would allow me to spend more time with my family.

That's the moment I transitioned from corporate sales into the investment world. I opened my own office and partnered with one of the top brokerages in the nation. Taking this major step led to some immediate improvements in my life. I was home every evening and every weekend. There were no more weeks traveling to faraway towns without my wife or my kids. But there were downsides as well. In particular, the brokerage that I was registered with had some very strict requirements. They didn't believe there was much value in picking up the phone and cold calling potential clients. Instead, they insisted that I personally go to people's houses, knock, and have a conversation with whoever opened the door. I was required to log the names of at least twenty-five people I talked to—every single day.

For some, this would probably not be a big deal, perhaps it might even be a part of the job they looked forward to. For me, it was torture. Like Brooke, I am by nature a bit of an introvert, and I hated those first few months of awkward conversations.

The word "hate" is not an exaggeration. I hated knocking on doors so much, I wasted as much time as possible getting ready for work, driving from one area of town to another, and seeking the perfect parking spot, all in an effort to avoid the inevitable. The very thought of the work made me physically ill. I was throwing up every single morning. I lost twenty pounds the first nine months I was there.

No matter how much I hated it, though, I had to get the work done. And I did for three years—because I knew *why* I was doing it. And that made all the difference.

WHY POWERS YOUR EFFORTS

In my work as a life coach, I have noticed a trend. Young men often don't know *why* they do any of the things they do. They can tell the *what* they do but not *why* do it. Most of us have good reasons for becoming entrepreneurs. We have good reasons for getting married. And we have good reasons for having children. Yet, in our day-to-day lives, we lose track of those reasons. We work because we're supposed to work. If we think about it at all, the reason is to make money or to grow the business. We have a family because we wanted one, and it just sort of felt like the right thing to do. And we keep trying to be a good family man because we love the people who make up that family. End of story.

This is what I call living on default. You keep doing things because that's what you do. You don't look for deeper reasons or motivations. Living on default can lead to problems when things are all going well, but it raises particular problems if you're struggling to find balance between your commitments to your family and your company.

In the first place, without a clear *why*, it's a lot easier to quit—even the things you really care about. Whether it's climbing a mountain, running a marathon, starting a business, keeping a marriage going, or raising kids, the work required to succeed is immense, and there are going to be plenty of opportunities to give up. Giving up doesn't always look like shutting down a business or getting a divorce. It can be a slow process of putting in less effort toward any one of your priorities.

In the years ahead, there will be nights when you have a big meeting the next day and your child gets sick and needs your attention all night. There will be days when you come home from a tough day and instead of receiving support, you have to give it to your spouse. Without a *why*, it can be hard to keep trying to get these moments right.

At the same time, living without a *why* can be hard to find the motivation that is key to improvement and success in any of your ambitions. I grew up seeing the power of *why* in action in my mother's career. Mom was a teacher, and she and her colleagues put everything into their work. They'd put their own money into supplies. They'd stay after to talk to students. They did it because they knew *why* they were in that profession. They knew the work mattered. They knew that this would be the only safe place where those kids could learn and grow. And so they were always willing to do more.

Despite the obvious value of such clear motivation, young men often concentrate too much on *how* we're going to do everything and too little on *why* we make the effort. Don't get me wrong; how is important. *How* will make up most of the rest of this book, but *why* deserves some focus first because *why* is how we take ourselves out of default, recognize what we truly want, and find the capacity to achieve it all.

There's a young entrepreneur in our agency, we will call him "Materialistic Guy," who comes to me for coaching. Materialistic Guy is about to have another child, but despite the need to tighten the family budget, he keeps spending money on material stuff for himself. Last year, he bought himself a fancy car, then he traded that in and bought, in his words, "a big badass pickup."

I couldn't understand his thinking on these choices. Why was he working himself to the bone and missing time with his family all so he could buy fancy vehicles? Were those cars really more important than everything else in his life? So I pulled him aside and asked him to explain what was up with the rigs. I asked him a very simple question: why?

He didn't have an immediate answer. Sure, he had words to say—about the need to build the business, how he needed to look successful, and how great the truck was—but he didn't really address the main question. He couldn't tell me the deeper reason he was making these choices.

But Materialistic Guy didn't give up. He kept thinking the question over, and when he called me a couple weeks later, he finally had a real answer.

"Pat," he said, "The truth is, the thing I want more than anything—my *why*—is that I want things to be different than they were for me growing up. My dad worked all the time, but we never had much money. That's why I'm working so hard. I guess I buy myself cars to prove to myself that I'm getting closer to that goal."

"That's a really noble goal," I told him, "But you've been so focused on work and buying stuff that you're missing all the time you should be spending with your kids. You don't want them growing up missing their dad all the time, do you?"

He'd never thought of it that way. Of course he hadn't. Materialistic Guy hadn't really thought of any of the consequences of his choices—he'd been on default for years. It was only once he'd focused on finding his *why* that his priorities began to fall into place. That *why* clarified what he really wanted and what his real responsibilities were.

The same was true for me. When I was walking those neighborhoods, knocking on doors to find the clients that would help me build my new business, I needed to really understand *why* I was doing this to myself. Why was I torturing myself every morning doing something I hated?

For me, it all came down to my family. In the first place, I was deeply motivated by the retirement struggles my mother and my step-father, John, had faced. Their financial trouble began with her retirement. Having put thirty years of work and sacrifice into her students, my mom decided in the late '80s that it was finally time to retire. For all that time and effort, though, the only retirement money she had was her teacher's pension. It was extremely important that she make the right choices about that pension—but she didn't realize that.

Instead of speaking to someone with the financial understanding to explain her options fully, Mom sat down with a teacher friend and the school custodian to puzzle out the options. They had no idea what they were doing, so they just chose the highest number available on the form, she signed it and sent it in. Little did they know that that choice would mean John would not receive a cent from that pension if my mother passed before him.

The situation soon got worse. John didn't have a pension, but he had invested his money—slowly buying up stock in the company he ran. John's business was handling the logistics between the farm and the store. Farmers would drop their produce at his warehouse, and John would contract with buyers around the world to sell it. At the time of my mother's retirement, he owned 48 percent of that company. But that wasn't enough to stop what happened next. Two years after my mom's retirement, two gentlemen walked into John's office and told him they now owned the majority of the company. And that meant they were his bosses. It took those men only two more years to drive the business into the ground. They declared bankruptcy, and in the process, threw away John's entire savings.

My parents were at the top of my mind in creating my business. Not only did I believe that I was doing a public good helping people avoid making the mistakes my parents had, I also knew that my success would mean that John never had to worry if my mother passed first. I would be able to help financially.

The *why* behind my business helped get me out of bed every morning, but it was the *why* behind my young family that kept me going from door to door.

To remind myself of that *why*, I made myself a little picture book. The book had an eagle soaring on the cover and underneath it had the word "Goals." Inside, I had five pictures. Each page had room for five checks—twenty-five checks in total for the twenty-five people I needed to talk to each day.

If I could check all five checks on all five pages, I would be done with that task and could get back to the office.

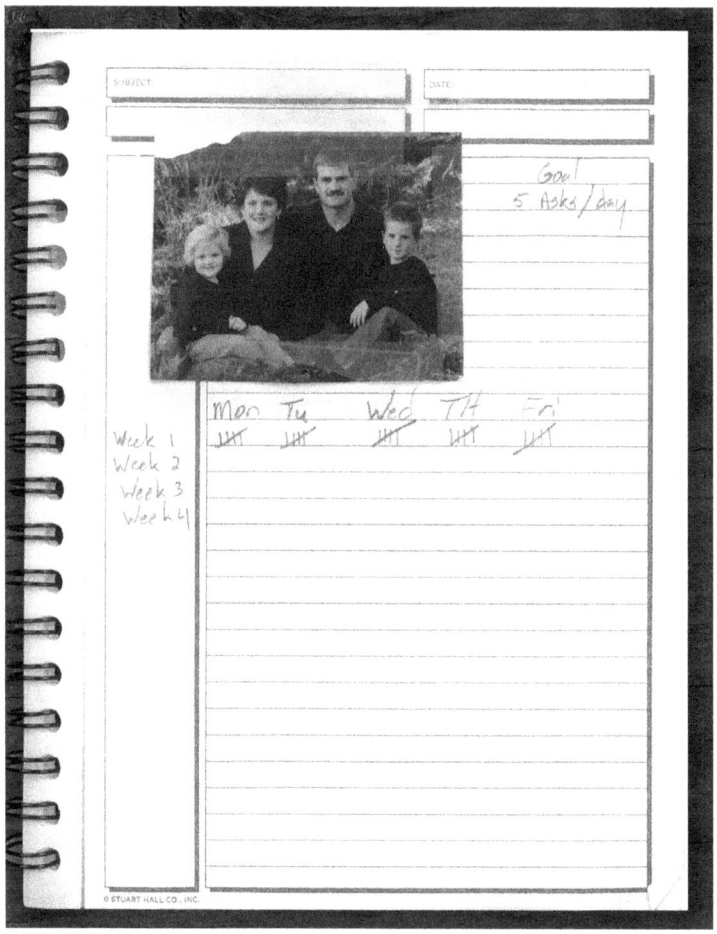

On the first page was a picture of my wife and kids. Having the whole family there made those first five checks—the hardest ones to motivate myself to get—a lot easier. The next page was a picture of just my son, Bryce. Then there was one of Morgan, my precious newborn. The last two pages were for me. On the fourth page was a picture of a jet boat that was capable of navigating the whitewater of Hell's Canyon. The last picture was a picture of a caribou because I dreamed of going caribou hunting in the Arctic.

The way this was organized brought me further clarity. The main *why* behind my actions was my family. Those personal, selfish motivations came last. I had to do this for my family first, and only if I found enough success to take care of them could I do those fun things for me.

FINDING YOUR *WHYS*

Clearly, setting down a *why* offers a lot of value. But how do you go about finding your own *why*?

In the first place, this isn't a matter of developing a single *why* that covers your whole life. My own *whys* included a desire to help John and to prevent others from experiencing what my parents were going through, the desire to be a good family man who is always there for his family and takes care of them, and my own interest in enjoying my time hunting and exploring nature.

And that was only the beginning. My *whys* also included a focus on my health because it is important to me that I am physically fit and able to enjoy long treks out in the woods and a good workout to blow off some steam.

You also need a *why* in place for everything that is important to you. Why did you start your business and why do you keep working at it? Why did you get married and why do you want that marriage to last? Why did you have kids and what influence do you want to have over them?

In each case, you have to dig deeper than the obvious answers. I know you started a business partly because you wanted to make money and you wanted that extra freedom. That's true of every entrepreneur. But what if we remove those carrots? What do you have left? If we put aside the money and the freedom, why do you do what you do?

The answer could be anything. You could feel fulfilled in the work itself, or feel you're doing good for the world in your position—even if it's in a small way. You could love the clients or your employees. But there has to be something beyond money and the potential to someday take extra vacation days.

The same is true for your marriage. The immediate *why* for your relationship is obvious: you love your spouse. You are raising a family together. But that isn't deep enough. You need to consider what you find valuable within that relationship. Lay out what you like about this person. If you put aside the stress and conflict that come from raising young kids, what is it you enjoy about the person you married?

Is it the fact that they make you laugh or that they always understand where you're coming from? Is it your shared interests or the way they can make you think or how they come up with ideas you've never considered before?

Simply getting these *whys* out can often go a long way towards improving that relationship. The *why* can replace your default settings that are stuck on inertia and avoiding conflict at all costs. It can help you focus on what you love about this relationship.

And then there are your kids. In some ways, this seems like the easiest *why* to settle. On some level, the reason behind almost everything you do for your kids is that you love them. It's as innate and natural as breathing. But once again, we have to dig deeper. What do you love about your children? What do you like about their personalities? Why do you want to have more time with them or a stronger relationship? And just as importantly, what kind of person do you want to help them become? What kind of relationship do you want with them not just today but in twenty years?

Pushing beyond the default answer of love removes a lot of the excuses we give ourselves for putting our kids second. My father loved us, and I'm sure that love was part of his reasoning for all that extra work he took on. It wasn't until decades later that he realized he'd let his work ambitions push the *why* of his fatherhood aside. Only when it was too late did he recognize that he had an intense desire for a strong relationship with his sons.

If you want to avoid the sort of path my father followed, you need to set yourself on a new one now, and that starts with recognizing why you want things to be different—for you, your work, your spouse, and your kids. And more. There's no need to stop listing *whys* on that list. I have a *why* for my health. There's a *why* behind my friendships, and a *why* for my hobbies. There's no limit to your introspection here. But you do need to get the big *whys* down first—because they will help you determine what real success means in your life.

IDENTIFY SUCCESS

Getting off of default and developing your *whys* has still more to offer—because *why* can also help you determine what success actually means—for you, your business, and your family.

Entrepreneurs very rarely ask themselves two very important questions:

"When have I succeeded?"

"When do I have enough?"

Because most entrepreneurs are on default, they have no answer for these questions. In fact, many entrepreneurs feel that they shouldn't have answers to such questions. There is no "enough," and "success" is only temporary—a step up an ever-rising ladder. But without answers, you never know when you can take your foot off the pedal, when you can relax, or when you can celebrate. You can never decide when to give yourself a break or put something else first—no matter how far you've come or how much you've achieved.

Once again, this isn't just about business. You also need answers to these questions in your marriage and with your kids. I had items in my "Goals" book that were just for me because it's important to take care of yourself and enjoy things for yourself. When are you willing to give yourself time for what you care about? Alternatively, if you're more like Materialistic Guy and jump at opportunities to reward yourself, have you done enough to earn those personal rewards? Have you taken enough care of your family that you deserve that new big pickup or Mercedes?

Luckily, you can answer these questions now that you have your *whys*.

If your *why* for business is the atmosphere in your office, do you really have to grow 20 percent each year to enjoy the company culture you've built? Would growing at 18 or 15 or even 10 percent for a year or two and spending more time with your family affect your relationship with the employees you care about? Wouldn't that only improve the company culture that you love?

If the *why* behind your marriage is a shared love of going to the movies and long discussions into the night, are you making enough time to enjoy those evenings regularly? What could you change to make more of those evenings happen?

If you are really driven to raise your children to value hard work and the contribution everyone can make to society, are you putting in the time to teach them those values and to create a bond in which they trust your judgment on such matters?

Far too often, we expect entrepreneurs to be unsatisfied workaholics who always drive themselves to do *more* with their business. But that is not a happy way to live—for you, your employees, your spouse, or your kids. And it isn't natural. Even the most driven athletes know how to set goals, celebrate when they achieve them, and take time off to live their lives. These are almost inhumanly driven, hard-working individuals, but when they win the Super Bowl or the Indy 500, they don't go back to the gym the next day. They take time to enjoy it.

And even the greatest athletes recognize when they've done enough and call time on their careers.

So what does "success" and "enough" look like for you for each of your *whys*?

As you formulate these points, I want you to keep a couple things in mind. First, be sure to test how firm your "enough" is. If one of your *whys* is to make enough to live in the best neighborhood in town and go on the best vacations, could you see yourself being satisfied with the second-best neighborhood or vacations in Florida instead of Maui. Could that be *good enough*—especially if it meant fulfilling a more important *why*, like spending more quality time with your family?

Or, once you have the best house and regularly go on amazing vacations, would you be willing to step back and lower that *why* on your priority list? Could you see any further success as a cherry on top that deserves less of your immediate attention?

Second, it's important to recognize success across a spectrum of positive improvements. If your most important *why* is family, it is a success every time you make it out of the office and get to your child's ball game. It's a success every time you rearrange things at work so you can have breakfast with the kids or get lunch with your spouse.

These are not huge wins, but they are wins, and you should celebrate them. You may not deserve the new fancy vehicle for a lunch date, but you deserve to feel good about yourself for it. Society isn't giving men a lot of rewards for being good family men, so we have to treat ourselves well.

Along the same lines, you should recognize and celebrate the big successes for what they are. If you and your spouse make it through a tough year, that next anniversary is a huge win. That means you should do more than just go to dinner like you always do. You should go all out. You and your spouse should celebrate—big time! Pull out all the stops the same way you would if you hit 25 percent growth in one year.

Setting clear ideas of "enough" and celebrating "success" on every level is about more than giving yourself a break and having some fun. With these standards in place, you can better channel your energy into what matters and know when you can move on to the next responsibility—and that will only help you run your business better and be a better father and husband.

WHY LEADS TO MORE SUCCESS

Having a set of *whys* can make you a far better entrepreneur, husband, and dad. It can also make you a better leader and manager. A leader who lives their life on default and only values money will make less than a leader that has a *why* that includes helping others develop and reach their goals. In other words, default only hurts your business and your family. *Why* helps you succeed in both.

This was certainly true for me. Thanks to clarifying my priorities, I eventually improved enough at the door-to-door game that I would sign a new client every single day. I even got an award for prospecting. I became known in that community as "the walking stockbroker."

It wasn't that I was a particularly brilliant door-to-door salesperson. I simply had the drive to stick with it and perfect the work. I knew why I was doing it, and that allowed me to become a success at it—all while focusing on finding ever more time for my family.

My *why* has also been crucial in allowing me to be a success for my parents. At this point, I know I'll be able to take care of my parents, if they should ever need it. (Although, he and my mother are both still living and doing fine without much help!)

Likewise, Materialistic Guy has finally begun seeing more success on what matters most to him. Recently, he called me to tell me his third child is almost due. During the call, he pointed out how tired he was.

"I tell you, Pat, I'm burning the candle at both ends. Every evening I'm taking care of my wife and kids. I'm so focused on it, I'm having to work less."

I'm sure he expected me to commiserate with him—or to push him to get back to work as others no doubt had already—but that's not the reaction he got. Instead, I told him how awesome that sounded.

"What?" he said in confusion. "It's awesome that I might lose some business?"

"Well, are you going to go broke?" I asked.

"No."

"Is the business at risk? Did you have to let anyone go?"

"No," he admitted, "but we're not going to hit our targets."

"Then, congratulations," I said. "You are making the right choices!"

That was another important lesson for Materialistic Guy—who is not so materialistic these days. Not only did he need a *why* to show him what mattered, he needed to recognize what mattered most. It was time to put his most important client first. And that wasn't the person spending the most at his company; it was the family waiting for him at home.

CHAPTER 4

FAMILY IS YOUR MOST IMPORTANT CLIENT

WHEN I STARTED IN THE INVESTMENT BUSINESS, I KNEW there was a lot of work ahead—not just knocking on doors but also building up a team and serving the clients I brought in the office. But my number one concern wasn't those dreaded doors or the currently empty client lists I'd have to fill in; it was breakfast.

Breakfast, as we've all been told a million times, is the most important meal of the day. I absolutely agree with this, and not just for health reasons. I think it's important for a family to start the day together at the table over a meal. It's easy to grab a bite and rush out the door, but having a little time together reminds everyone of that familial bond before the stresses of the day take over.

I believe so much in this that breakfast was one of the *whys* behind my decision to start my own company. And once I did, I committed to the idea. Every morning, I got up with my kids, made them breakfast, and took them to school. Because Brooke wasn't her own boss, she often had to leave early for her work, so it became my responsibility and my privilege to cook up a healthy meal to help the kids get off to school well.

The general partner for our region from the national brokerage my company partnered with, Corporate Guy, didn't understand this. And he made his opinions about this practice very clear. He made a habit of calling from the office at six each morning. If I didn't pick up—because I never picked up the phone that early—he'd leave voice-mails.

"The market is open, I've already made $10,000. Why aren't you in the office yet?"

"I've just made another sale. You should be here by now."

"Tick tock. Time to get to work, Pat."

The calls would continue until I got into the office.

To be clear, the problem wasn't my numbers—which were very strong—or the growth of my company. I very quickly entered the top tier of financial advisors in the area. But I wasn't number one. I wasn't willing to outwork every single advisor and grab every single dollar on the table. And it drove Corporate Guy crazy. He simply couldn't understand why I wasn't willing to put everything else aside to make that extra sale at six in the morning.

He felt I should be living my life around the office, and he couldn't let it go.

One day, I came into my office and saw him sitting in my chair, demanding to know why I was late. If I hadn't had my priorities straight, this bullying might have had an effect. I might have relented and compromised—coming in early a couple days a week or offering to stay later. But I knew not just why I was making my choices but which *whys* should come first if push came to shove. So when Corporate Guy shoved, I shoved right back.

"Listen," I told him, "I make my children breakfast every morning, and I take them to school. Every morning. If you don't like it, I'm ready to walk away from working with your company. I went into this business because I wanted to be the master of my own schedule. If I can't have that mastery while working with you, I'm ready to leave and find a partner who understands this."

From that point on, the calls stopped. I put my foot down on my priorities, and I won those stress-free breakfasts with my kids.

THE "TAKE A BULLET" TEST

In the last chapter, we considered the value of creating a set of *whys* for everything that matters in your life. This is a powerful way to capture and understand your motivations. But as entrepreneurs, we live busy lives with immense responsibilities that constantly pull at us in conflicting directions. You may know *why* you want to do it all, but at some point, decisions have to be made about which *whys* get priority.

Part of the difficulty of balancing the roles of being a family man and running a business is not knowing that everything is important but choosing what is the *most* important at any particular moment.

To help clarify what should get priority in your life, let me ask you a question: what would you take a bullet for? Would you take a bullet for your business? Would you take a bullet for your current income level? In other words, are you willing to die for your company or your paycheck?

Probably not. But I bet you would take a bullet for your family. You'd sacrifice anything to keep them healthy, safe, and happy. And knowing that shows you what your priorities should be. After all, if you are willing to take a bullet for your family, shouldn't you be willing to leave for work thirty minutes later so you get a little more time with them every day? Shouldn't you be willing to put work aside and pay direct attention to the people who you are willing to die for?

Like your *whys*, the "take a bullet" test helps overcome the default assumptions we have about how we should organize our lives and why we make the choices we do. I don't know how many times I've heard men tell me that they are working so hard and for so many hours because they are "doing it for the family." It's only when I challenge them on this and dig into it that we discover the actions don't live up to the explanation.

Setting priorities matters in business and family. Corporate Guy was right that I could have brought more money into my company by coming into the office earlier. At the same time, as we've already covered, if you aren't spending time taking care of your kids, you are literally putting them more in harm's way. By skipping breakfasts and coming home late every night, you are making it more likely they stumble into difficulties and tragedies later in life. These are statistically proven facts.

While the stakes feel low on a day-to-day basis, there's a clear choice you are making here, and what you care about most should help determine your decisions.

If you skipped mornings and weekends and birthdays to build a business and make enough money for your daughter to go to Harvard—but she ends up pregnant at fifteen and never goes to college, did you really put her first? If you're increasing that risk, why are you working so much? There are only two possible answers: either you didn't realize you were putting work first, or work truly is more important to you than your family.

If you're willing to take that bullet, you have to be just as willing to put the effort in, day after day, to give your children and your spouse the best possible future—with the most love and attention you can afford. It's less glamorous, but it's going to mean more to them later. And that should be your priority, *if* your family really is the most important thing in your life.

HOW DO YOU TREAT A VIP?

Making family a constant priority is a challenge. You have so many other responsibilities—to clients, to employees, to business partners, to investors. And that doesn't even touch on your responsibilities to friends, various associations you belong to, or your religious organization. Or the responsibilities you have to yourself. With so many commitments, it can be difficult to see how family can always come first, no matter how much you wish it were otherwise.

Before addressing this point directly, let's take a moment to recognize what should be obvious: you are not a failure for struggling with this dilemma. It is indeed a difficult problem. It's so difficult, in fact, that we will spend the remainder of Part II resolving it. And even once you have strategies in place to reduce the tension between your various responsibilities, you will still inevitably get the balance wrong sometimes.

With that said, we can definitely make some improvements, and to do that, we have to start by shifting your current mindset about what priority looks like at home.

Think about how you treat the most important client at your business. When they call you right before you leave the office, you take the call. If they need you to fly out somewhere for a discussion, you fly out. If they need something when you are on vacation or during a family holiday, you find a way to fit them in. And you always maintain contact.

In my business, we're required to remain in regular communication with our VIPs—assuming they want those check-ins. Beyond those frequent calls, emails, or mailers, though, if a VIP calls the office because they are feeling nervous about the market, I jump on the call and ease their minds. I would never tell them that because we talked last Tuesday, I can't make time for them on Monday. I make the time because they're *very important*.

Up to a point, there's no end to what most of us would do for the top clients in our businesses. I recently got a text from a VIP client that his friend was sick. He asked me to pray for this friend. I did so, and I made a point of supporting him emotionally as he went through a wearing period of worry.

That's what we do for our most important clients. We go the extra mile, every time.

So how would your behavior and choices change if you started seeing your family as your *most* important client—the client who should always get top priority over everyone else? After all, they're the ones you're willing to take a bullet for. You know they should come first—just like your top VIP. If you actually put them first, how would that change your relationship with your time and your responsibilities?

In the first place, you'd probably focus on communication more. If you touch base with a VIP client once a month, you've got to open the lines of communication every day with your family. You should touch base with every member, even if it's only a passing question about their day.

At the same time, when they need you, you'd step up. If your child is sick, you shouldn't leave it to your spouse to nurse them back to health, you should find time to do your part—even if that means putting other work off. If your kid is struggling with homework, you should take a few minutes to puzzle it out with them. The moments when they need emotional support—as my VIP client did recently—you would be there.

Finally, if your family were your most important client, you'd be sure to give them your full attention. After all, you don't sit in a meeting with a VIP staring at your phone or answer an email from another client when hearing about your VIP's trouble. You don't tell your VIP client that you're just too busy to have a ten-minute conversation today. So why do you feel that's okay when it comes to your children or your spouse?

When communicating, nursing, assisting, or listening to your spouse or your kids, you should put everything else aside—physically and mentally. The same way you make every effort to be present with your most important client, you should be present with your family.

This doesn't mean you have to spoil them. It doesn't mean that every minute of your life has to be devoted to them. But like your best clients, they deserve your attention, empathy, interest, assistance, and time. And their needs should come first.

SET EXPECTATIONS

To put action behind intention will require some significant realignment in your life. Above all, you need to be honest with your family and communicate what a potential change in priorities is going to look like—and exactly how far you can stretch your schedule and your energy to fit everything in.

What does your schedule look like if you start staying home for breakfast each morning? What does it look like if you take weekends off? How does that affect your income and the family budget? How might it affect retirement savings and plans? Does your family understand the potential sacrifices necessary to keep you home more often?

You don't have to poll the family to see exactly how much they want you home versus a new PlayStation. The key here is setting expectations at a reasonable level so you don't over-promise or under-deliver. If you leave your family assuming you can make breakfast *and* get home every evening in time to watch your kids play every game for their basketball team *and* keep the business growing *and* bring home the same amount of income—you are going to struggle and most likely fail to deliver on those assumptions. No father wants to admit that they can't do it all, but failing to deliver on those expectations is far worse than simply explaining your limitations. If you can't make all of that happen, you should be direct and clear with your family about why that is.

Think about this from your kid's perspective. Let's say your daughter has a big moment in a basketball game. She's been on the bench all season, trying her best to improve, and she finally gets the call to go in. She gets the ball with ten second left, she heaves it up at the basket, and she scores! She looks over to the stands, and you're not there.

That's heartbreaking, no matter what. But it's far more heartbreaking for her if you said you'd be at the game. If you told her last week that you had to work late on that day and when you got home, your first question is about the game, she can accept that situation. She will understand that you love her and care about her life. But if you said you'd be there and then miss the big moment? It's hard to heal that disappointment.

And don't think you can avoid conversation by simply bringing work with you. Again, it's far better for her to know Dad had to work than seeing Dad working on his computer when every other parent had their phones out filming her big moment.

The point is to set those expectations honestly and make genuine effort to always meet them.

This is not just hypothetical. I experienced those disappointed expectations with my father. I remember one Friday when my dad told Scott and I that we were going to go hunting the next day. We were so excited that we could barely sleep that night. We were going to go hunting with Dad! This was such a rare chance to really spend time with him.

The next morning, though, before we got to the woods, we stopped at another kid's house. What were we doing? It turned out, my dad had committed to taking someone else's son with us—someone, he told us, who didn't have an active father in his life.

"He needs some attention," we were told.

My main memory from that day is not hunting with my dad. It's feeling hurt and angry. There's an obvious mistake my dad made here, of course. He should have recognized that his sons needed attention, too. But it was nearly as bad that he failed to set expectations. If he had told us the day before that someone would join us on the trip, we wouldn't have been as excited that night but also wouldn't have been as let down. It wouldn't have gone down as one of the greatest trips of my life, but it also wouldn't remain a sore point in my memory today.

BECOME INTENTIONAL WITH YOUR CLIENT SELECTION

To serve your most important clients, communication and expectations have to extend beyond the family. To make the changes necessary, that flexibility and understanding has to be seen in the office and with your clients.

As the leader of your organization, you have a significant influence over who is on your team and the culture of your workplace. As we'll discuss more in the next chapter, you can set standards and organize your team to allow you to make that ballgame. If one of your employees doesn't like the adjustments you might make to achieve this, you can find someone more understanding.

Clients are more difficult. You can't always easily replace a difficult client or brush off their criticism of the hours you're keeping at work. If you're barely scraping by, you may have to work with some demanding people who don't offer you the respect and understanding you'd deserve—and that you require to really commit to your role as a father.

However, one of your business goals should be to get to a place in which you can choose to let those clients go and replace them with clients who can accommodate your needs.

How would you react if a client canceled for an unexpected family situation? You'd understand, of course. You'd tell them it was fine and reschedule. You'd be willing to talk to someone else in their office if that person could provide the same information you needed.

Your clients should afford you the same respect.

Keep in mind, you don't have to help everybody. You don't have to sign up every account and keep it forever. For those clients who get in the way of your family, you know now that family has to come first—as soon and as often as it can.

CREATING SPACE TO STEP AWAY

For all your careful planning and mindset shifts, chaos is inevitable when balancing a business and a family. Your kids will get sick at the very worst time. Your spouse will have to go out of town right before a big presentation. You'll have to miss some of those games because some task at work requires your immediate attention.

It's best to simply accept that now. But that doesn't mean all of this is pointless. By organizing your priorities, you have a far better idea of how you want to run your life. The next step is creating the space for that to be possible—most of the time.

Because I knew what I wanted from life, I was able to begin organizing my business to continue to grow even as I took more time for myself and my family. By the time I opened a new office with a different firm, Corporate Guy was bending over backward to convince me to stay. Of course he was—I was one of his higher producers. I was never the *top* producer the way he wanted, but my business had solid growth every year. And he didn't want to see that revenue disappear.

At the same time, I never had to miss those breakfasts. To this day, my kids look forward to the mornings I get up to make them Mickey Mouse waffles. Those mouse ears just bring happy memories of the times when Dad put them first.

I was able to fit it all in, but to do that, I had to lift up those in my office so that things could run smoothly while I was standing over the waffle iron. It was only once business could go on as usual without my constant supervision that I could really attend to my most important clients.

CHAPTER 5

LEARNING TO STEP AWAY

A COLLEAGUE OF MINE FROM A DIFFERENT OFFICE IN OUR building, "Workaholic Guy", fits every description of that definition. Workaholic Guy comes into the office at 6:30 every morning, and from that moment until he locks up in the evening, he's in control of every aspect of his office. If there's any business to do, he's in the office doing it.

The cost of these long hours has been pretty disastrous on his family life. He has a distant, frosty relationship with his wife and his children. But the connection between work and family doesn't appear to have ever crossed his mind. Far from recognizing the fault in dedicating his entire life to work, he chides others—in his office and outside it—to make the same choices he does.

That includes me. At some point, he started making a habit of commenting every time I came into the office later than him—which is almost every day. I'd seen his sort before. In this respect, he isn't so different from how Corporate Guy, who used to leave me demanding voicemails at my last company. And like Corporate Guy, Workaholic Guy's constant haranguing really started to wear on me.

On one particular day, Workaholic Guy waved me down in his typical fashion as I was heading for my office.

"Nice of you to show up, " he said, as he looked at his watch. "I've already been working for two hours."

"That's great," I told him, trying to get past. But he wouldn't let it go.

"You really ought to be here before seven each day. How can you expect your people to stay on top of their work if you aren't staying on top of them? How can you expect your clients to stick with you if you aren't sweating blood for them every single day?"

Perhaps there was something in his tone that reminded me of Corporate Guy's voicemails. Perhaps I was just tired and tired of listening to a workaholic bully. For whatever reason, that was the day I finally snapped back.

"If I had your money," I said, "I'd burn mine and retire."

He stopped in his tracks. I'd clearly surprised and confused him. He was offended, but he also seemed unable to quite grasp what I was criticizing.

"I could retire anytime I wanted," he responded, lamely.

"Good for you," I responded. "Work is not my life."

I let it go at that. There was no point trying to explain myself further. He'd made his life choices, and no words from me were ever going to shake his confidence that he'd chosen correctly. In fact, no evidence from his own life could upset the path he'd laid for himself. Not only was his family drifting away from him, he'd run his health into the ground. His employees were all either workaholics like him or burned out, disillusioned, and likely to quit at any moment.

He was right. He could retire anytime. But he was never going to. Because he had nothing else in his life. He'd never created the space for anything else. And he wasn't going to start now.

YOU ARE NOT YOUR BUSINESS

If you don't want to end up like my overworked, overconfident, bullying colleague, Workaholic Guy, with very little to go home to in the evening, you have to create space for the people you care about most: your biggest *why*, your most important clients—your family. To make that space you have to do more than recognize the importance of your VIPs at home; you have to reorganize your business so that you can step away from your office responsibilities and attend to your spouse and children.

This is obviously more complicated than simply snapping your fingers and deciding to come into work an hour later than you currently do. It requires more than a desire for a schedule that reflects the change in your mindset. To make this work, you have to implement some radical changes in your office.

It all starts with a change in the office culture. And to change that culture, you have to confront some often deeply cherished beliefs about your role in your business. Specifically, you have to be willing to make a concerted effort to make *your* business less about *you*.

Transitioning your business so you aren't the center of everything often feels quite unnatural to an entrepreneur. After all, this is the business *you* built. It's *your* creation. On some level, it feels like it should always be about *you*. However, before you can take a single practical step towards that increased focus on your family, you have to recognize that your business can still be yours even if you aren't center stage for every task and every decision. In fact, it can run *better* if you take yourself out of many parts of the process.

This self-sustaining office isn't always immediately possible. In the early days, when I was still getting my business up and running, it was all about me—because it had to be. If I didn't produce—knocking on those doors, setting up accounts in the office, taking every call, safeguarding every client's assets—I didn't get a paycheck. If I couldn't create growth myself, the business simply wasn't going to grow. The only way to earn enough revenue to hire more staff to take over some of those responsibilities was to generate it myself.

That was exhausting work, but it was also rewarding. Every new satisfied client came down to my own efforts. No one could say I wasn't the one building this new company.

To a certain extent, that perspective is necessary in the early days of entrepreneurship. In those early stages of entrepreneurship, you really do have to work a great deal because you don't have the people in place to take on more, and it helps to feel that pride in what you're creating. Perhaps that is where your business is now. In which case, you'll want to concentrate on modest changes in your schedule and communicating to your family that this is temporary.

Because it should be temporary. At a certain point, as your business begins to stabilize and the size of the team increases, the opportunity to do less should present itself. Unfortunately, that opportunity often runs up against the inclination to keep feeling that immediate pride of ownership when you are involved in everything. It's your company, and you want to know what everyone is doing. You want to call every shot.

Workaholic Guy never grew out of that perspective. He still sees his whole purpose as working harder than anyone and pushing everyone to try to keep up. He has to be involved in everything, and nothing else in his life is allowed to get in his way.

That's where our mindsets depart—and where yours should too. Once my business was established, I realized I had to focus on finding places where I could remove myself from the center of things enough that I could come in at 8:30 instead of 6:30 so I could have those breakfasts with my kids.

It required a sacrifice of some ego to organize my business in a way that opened my schedule, but it was absolutely worth it.

BUILDING A TEAM THAT CAN WORK WITHOUT YOU

Once you've accepted the need to remove yourself from the center of your business, you can start making that change a reality by finding the right people to take on that extra responsibility. This step is critical not only for your relationship with your family but also for the health of your business.

There's an African proverb, "If you want to fast, go alone. If you want to go far, go together." In other words, to build a business quickly, you need to take on everything yourself. When you want a business that continues to grow for years and gives you room for a life to go along with your success, you'll need a team to support you.

To create that team your first priority should be hiring a group of individuals who are all strongest where you are most limited. To even accept your limitations can be difficult, of course, and it can be equally tricky to hire for those limitations instead of trying to improve in those areas yourself. That's certainly the most common advice for entrepreneurs out there these days. I don't know how many classes I've been to that focus on teaching entrepreneurs how to be better at what they naturally do poorly.

But the philosophy behind making yourself the best at everything is also the philosophy that requires you to be in the office 24/7. Besides, it doesn't make a ton of sense. If I were putting together a track and field team and I happened to be a great sprinter but a poor distance runner, why would I spend extra time and effort training for a marathon? Wouldn't it be wiser to focus my efforts on becoming an even greater sprinter and add a natural distance runner to my team?

When you hire others to lift the load where you're weakest, you can lift the company higher because you can focus on making the biggest possible impact in the areas you're most exceptional.

For instance, I am very good at making in-person connections. I struggle more with making calls and organizing paperwork. It's just not where I'm strongest. Once I was in a position to hire a team, I focused on finding people who were much better in those areas. Now I can step into more in-person meetings because someone with a different skillset is going to make the scheduling calls and draw up the contracts.

Once you've filled your office with people who add new strengths to the team, you can move on to hiring others to reinforce your strengths. After all, a racecar driver may also excel at changing tires, but if he hops out of the car at every pitstop to change his own wheels, he's not going to win any races. He's just wasting time when he could be doing what he does best: racing.

In your own work, you may prove excellent at any number of tasks, but a well-run organization requires others to take on most of the responsibility so you can concentrate on the big picture items that really move the company forward. Your job is to win that race—and then get home to your family. You need a team that can handle everything so you create success at home and in the office.

And that *team* element shouldn't be underestimated—which is why skills shouldn't be your only consideration when hiring a team. As you hire for your office, you also want to look for people who are hardworking, decent, and good team players. It'll do you no good to have a superior personal assistant who alienates all the other talented individuals in your office, leaving you to pick up the pieces when each team member departs one after another.

CREATE A CULTURE OF INDEPENDENCE

Though I suggested that ego is the central reason entrepreneurs have their work-life balance so skewed, I know that isn't always the case. Many entrepreneurs aren't in the office all the time because they want to be the center of attention. They may accept that things *should* run without them and even hire people to run things without them, but as soon as they walk out the door, they get a call from their team with a question that requires their immediate attention.

Imagine if you skipped a day at work in order to go on a field trip with your kid, what would happen in the office? Could your team handle all their regular tasks without you? Could someone step up to take on your standard responsibilities for the day? What if an important client called with a big question—could someone in the office answer it? Or would they have to call you?

Hiring your team using the criteria above can free up your resources while you're in the office, but a good team doesn't necessarily free up your time to be away from work. To do that, you have to foster a culture of independence.

Creating that culture of independence is a two-fold process. In the first place, you have to take that team filled with unique strengths and train them to take on overlapping responsibilities. These overlapping responsibilities should include everyone's tasks, including yours. One person may handle all your calling needs, but what do you do if that person is sick? Who handles the calls then? You don't need to double train for each role, but each person in the office should be able to expand their duties to pick up the slack when someone is out.

This is how you create the space to step away. There may not be one individual person who can do all that you do or make all the decisions you make, but the team as a whole should be able to handle everything but emergencies when you're out of the office.

If you want to encourage these overlapping responsibilities, you also need to make sure each person feels trusted, independent, and free to make some mistakes. Instead of standing over everyone and checking their work, once a person has been trained and has proven they know their duties, trust them to get the work done in the manner that works best for them.

Whatever their process, so long as the work is done well, you should trust them to deliver for you. For instance, my primary assistant is in at seven most mornings. I don't set that expectation for her. But she knows that if she gets the work done early, she can leave earlier and spend more time with her own family and on her own interests. That works just fine for me, and she thrives on that extra independence.

As you expand that trust with their growing responsibilities, be sure you don't punish good-faith errors. If a call doesn't get returned because the person learning to cover reception responsibilities is still getting a handle on the phone system along with their regular work, be forgiving of the mistake and assist with further training.

Allow for growing pains as things transition and eventually everyone will grow comfortable with the new expectations—and the new freedoms those expectations present to everyone.

SHARE THE BENEFITS WITH YOUR TEAM

With a company that allows them to do what they do well, how they like to do it, and then trusts them to do it right, you are likely to instill a culture of fulfillment and pride in your office. People like my primary assistant will make the adjustments necessary to handle their work and expand their capabilities because they are working in their strongest areas and enjoy the benefits of the trust you place in them.

That's the final component of a culture that allows you to step away. As you begin to see opportunities to get away, be sure to share those benefits with others. It's a powerful motivator, and it also helps the whole company succeed. Simon Sinek (author of *Start with Why*) speaks of Southwest Airlines and how the prioritization of employee satisfaction has a trickle-down effect that leads to happier customers and happier shareholders. The business functions better because the people within the business are happier.

So share this new wealth of free time with all who deserve it. You need to be able to take time for your family, and so does your team. Recently, another one of my team members asked for three Fridays off in a row. Her twelve-year-old daughter had hockey games each week, and she wanted to travel to each one and cheer her child on. I immediately agreed to give her the time off—not only because she deserved it for all her hard work but because I knew she'd come in on Mondays happier and ready to put in the effort needed.

That's the power you have in your hands. Not only to create time for your family but to create time for the families of your people. And once you give them that opportunity, they'll be more than willing to pick up the slack so you get those hours with your family.

Then all you have to do is take the time. And that requires you to put those family priority moments on the calendar—so you never miss them.

Chapter 6

MAKE THE MOST OF YOUR TIME

Every Thursday, Brooke and I go out for lunch. For the better part of a decade, that lunch has been the first thing on my calendar each week. There are inevitably a number of meetings, deadlines, and other responsibilities that fill in the rest of my hours on my work days, but almost nothing is ever allowed to touch that one hour I set aside for Thursday lunch.

That lunch has come to be one of the highlights of my week. It's something I get to look forward to from Monday onward. Whether things are going well or not in the office, there's always that hour with Brooke. Sometimes, we make it an adventure. We might look for a new restaurant to try.

Brooke has an app that suggests new places based on our previous lunches. Ideally, we look for some hole-in-the-wall, local place that most people have never heard of.

Other times, when the weather is nice, we take the food to go and have a picnic in the park.

Indoor or outdoor, local or chain, for that lunch, my time belongs entirely to Brooke. Unless we have a big event to plan, I leave my phone in the car. Whatever is happening at work can wait until after we've had a moment to ourselves to catch up on our weeks. This is our time to talk about the kids, how work is going, and the various interests we share.

It's a single moment in a very busy week that we schedule just for ourselves.

TIME SHOWS CARE

The value of those lunches isn't just the actual interaction—although that is incredibly important—it's also the gesture itself. The very act of making that time a priority tells Brooke that I value her. Nothing communicates that you care about someone as straightforwardly as pushing aside everything else to focus on them.

It took me time to learn this lesson. There were periods earlier in our marriage when I would cancel meals with Brooke, or with the whole family, because I had something else to do. I had to see a client; I had to work on a particular investment. Whatever it was, I had something that I felt had to come before the most important people in my life.

And just as setting aside that time communicated importance, so did the act of pushing my family aside for something else. The message I was sending—and that you send every time you take a family event off your calendar—is that the other person or event or responsibility is more important than the people waiting for you at home. Sometimes, these delays or cancellations are inevitable. When a major client or investor requires your time, you have to give it, after all. But when you make this choice for big and small responsibilities in your business over months and years, those disruptions become much harder to justify.

You may never be able to make every single family meal, but you have to focus on making sure the missed dinners are much less common than the ones you actually attend. Luckily, with the right mindsets and a team in place to handle work when you're away, improving that balance should now be possible—so long as you become an expert at managing your calendar. You have to stop trying to squeeze in every meeting and start putting your family on that calendar, so that when an event or a meal pops up, you're there for it.

Only once you book the time and make the events can you take on any of the other recommendations in this book to strengthen the relationships in your family. If you don't find time every week for your spouse and your kids, you simply can't get to know them and get close to them the way you want to.

In that way, nothing is more important than your calendar. So get your calendar out now.

BOOK TIME FOR EVERYTHING

Do you have your calendar app open? Good, because scheduling time for your family goes well beyond getting in a single lunch with your spouse. You have to create time for everyone. That includes time with your spouse, time for each kid, and time for your whole family together. Depending on your relationships, you may also want to fit in time with your parents or in-laws.

This isn't the limit of your scheduling needs, either. You also need to set aside time for yourself. Often, when we're busy, personal time is the first thing to go. You might feel selfish or like you're wasting an hour or an evening if it is just doing something for you. Shouldn't you be working or getting quality time with someone?

But self-care is not selfish. It's critical if you want to keep up with the demands of being a father, husband, and entrepreneur. If you aren't taking care of your physical and mental health, the machine that is your body and mind will eventually break down. You will get sick; you will become exhausted; you may even become depressed.

You need time to recharge. That time will look differently for everyone, but it should include a healthy dose of activities you find personally fulfilling and people outside your family who can provide you with support.

So while it might be the first item on your new calendar, time for rest and your own interests absolutely should be on there. As should time with friends. That's part of finding the family-business balance as much as fitting in work and your relations.

MAKING THE MOST OF OFFICE TIME

With time strictly set aside for each member of your family, plus time with friends and time for yourself, an obvious question arises: How do you cram all of this into a week already filled with the responsibilities of work?

Sure, sometimes, these moments can overlap. Perhaps some of your family time is spent visiting the grandparents on some weekends, and when the kids fall asleep watching TV with Grandpa, you might be able to sneak off for an hour to get in a quick pick-up game. Perhaps you can go with your family to the zoo and tag team with your spouse to get individual time with each kid on that outing. However, you absolutely should not try to cram every interaction into a single brief period just to mark "family time" off your list of to-dos. Your family will notice if you're trying to rush through your time with them to get back to work each week. And your body and mind will also notice if you're short-changing them regularly.

Making this schedule more workable isn't about combining; it's about maximizing. You have to use your time well in every circumstance. And for an entrepreneur that starts with your time in the office.

Thanks to the changes in your hiring and culture, your limitations and even some of your strengths should now be covered by your team. That opens the door for you to fully concentrate on doing what you do best in your work and whatever pushes the company forward most effectively.

Wherever you make the most impact, be sure to fill as many of your work hours as possible with those tasks.

In particular, you want to concentrate on taking the lead on your best leads. When I was going door-to-door seeking new clients, I knew I needed a better way to make the most of that time. I wasn't enjoying the work, so I tried to find the homes most likely to sign up with sizable accounts. As Thomas J. Stanley puts it in *The Millionaire Next Door*, I learned the value of fishing where the bigger fish are located.

I had a whole city I could visit to find my best clients. You might have a whole state or the whole country—or even the whole world. Regardless of the market size or characteristics, Stanley shows that it's always best to focus your energy on finding the pond where the biggest fish are biting. Instead of casting your line in any old waterhole and hoping for a big catch, you'll achieve far more far faster if you put yourself in the right place.

The pond with the big fish isn't always the obvious one. In my case, the folks who were most likely to be interested in my services and to have a lot of money to invest were not the ones living in big houses with brand-new cars. It was the folks on the less flashy side of town with the smaller, all-brick homes and the Buicks in the driveway. The flashy families were often in debt, but those brick homes often housed people in a very strong financial position. That's where the responsible folks who could use some extra guidance were living. And that's where I found most of my best clients—in far less time than it would have taken in the fancier neighborhoods.

The same will be true in your business. There will be a profile that the majority of your best clients fit. If you concentrate your efforts on those who share the same profile, you're more likely to see more income and more growth coming in faster—even as you work fewer hours.

USING FAMILY TIME WELL

You don't just want to maximize your work time, you want to maximize the rest of your time as well. That means limiting how much of your time you're wasting and being present in all of your important activities.

How much time do you think you spend zoning out looking at the internet or TV each evening? Some of this time is well-spent—particularly when you're reading a great article or watching one of your favorite shows—but a lot of it is just wasted. Think of all you could accomplish if you took even half of that time and put it toward working out, taking up a hobby, or getting in some of that quality time with a member of your family.

Your commitments to yourself and your family don't have to be especially long. Perhaps, in some cases, it's as little as thirty minutes or an hour. But you need to make that time count.

When one of your important clients comes in to see you, you put your phone away. You don't stare at social media or contact another client while they're explaining their difficulties. You remain present and attentive with them. You should be the same way with your family.

That doesn't mean you can never have the phone out. Some days, you need a break, and that's okay. But such days should be the exception, not standard practice. On almost every evening, the phone should be put away so you can enjoy your time with the family.

Unfortunately, this is likely to require some real effort on your part. Most of us have become addicted to our technology. I was recently out at dinner with my mother-in-law. At the next table there was a large family, and every single one of them was on a phone—from the parents down to the youngest child.

It's very easy to fall into a technology affair in which we put social media or streaming services before everything that really matters in our lives. Zoning out becomes the default. When we're tired, overworked, and overstressed, it's all the easier to fall into this temptation.

But we have to resist and focus on the people in front of us. They are the reason we are working so hard and adjusting our schedules.

DON'T BREAK IT, ADJUST IT

I don't want to paint an impossible picture of a perfectly balanced life with enough time in which work and family are never in conflict. To be honest, there are Thursdays when Brooke and I have to cancel our lunches. Recently, she had to go out of town to attend to some sick animals. And I missed another lunch date because I also had to travel for work.

However, when we do cancel, we don't simply "rain check" the event until some uncertain time in the near future. We immediately schedule another time together in the same week. We find a space on our calendars in the next few days when we can have that hour together.

For all the value that comes from defining your *whys*, elevating family to VIP status, empowering your team so you can step away, and putting your family on your calendar, time will get away from you sometimes. When that happens, though, you should communicate the reason you're canceling beforehand, and then you need to make every effort to find that time elsewhere in the week.

Again, time is your most precious gift for your family. It's the clearest way to communicate that you care and the best opportunity to build those strong relationships you want. It's only once you have the time for family that you can start to focus on what matters: building relationships of love, respect, and care.

Building those relationships requires another set of skills. And that's where we're heading next.

PART III

BUILDING BETTER RELATIONSHIPS

CHAPTER 7

KEEP YOUR STRESSES SEPARATE

WHEN BRYCE AND MORGAN WERE AROUND SIX AND NINE, life became incredibly stressful. Brooke was working full-time at a veterinarian clinic that was making her miserable. The owners demanded she work fourteen-hour shifts, and they forced her to upsell every customer who came in—all so they could squeeze out every possible dollar from the business. She hated it, and a short-time later, she would end up leaving that clinic—which would add a different kind of pressure to our family.

I wasn't doing much better. I was starting out on my own without a stable set of clients, so I had to work long hours as well, at least until I could become better established.

Our combined work stress would have been enough for any family to deal with, but there was more. We'd just built a new house in a new town, unsettling the kids and adding more financial pressure.

And all of this was occurring in the tense run-up to the 2007 financial crisis.

As you might expect, this high level of stress took its toll. I began experiencing major back pain. The pain was so bad and so debilitating that I could have filed a disability claim because of how it limited my ability to work—except I needed to put in those hours at the office to get the business up and running.

Brooke's unhappiness at work and the kids being kids was also leading to constant arguing in the evenings. I was often caught in the middle, refereeing disagreements and trying to de-escalate things after a long and painful day of work.

It was hell, to put it bluntly, and honestly, at that time, I no longer looked forward to going home at all. Every time I pulled into the garage, I could feel my body tensing up as I prepared for whatever shouting match was going on inside.

At some point, it all became too much. During one nasty disagreement between Brooke and the kids, I got frustrated and lost my temper. I began shouting. I slammed the door and walked out. I was almost ready to just quit. I don't know what I intended to quit in particular, but I knew I couldn't keep this up.

As I cooled down, I realized I wasn't handling my side of things very well. It was true that I couldn't keep this up, but that was because I wasn't dealing with my stress well enough. I couldn't handle the stress at home because I was already stressed out from work. I was also taking my family and financial stress and bringing it to work. I kept winding myself tighter and tighter without ever relieving the strain.

Of course it was too much to handle. Of course I was about to burst.

But my family needed me to help them de-escalate so we could handle the stress of this moment together. That meant I needed to enter our home in as calm a state as possible.

To achieve lower stress throughout my life would be a significant project, but my initial solution at that particular moment was a simple one. I hung a sticker from the garage door opener in my car that said "pray before entering." It was a reminder. Every time I went to open the garage door, I saw the sticker, and I took a moment to pray for a calm and clear mind. With just that one moment of quiet to myself, I found that I stopped dreading the stress inside. I could distance myself from the struggles at the office and put myself in the right frame of mind for the evening ahead.

And that allowed me to be a better father and a better husband as I walked in.

DON'T LET YOUR STRESSES MIX

Being an entrepreneur is stressful. Being a dad is stressful. So is being a husband. Reorganizing your office and disrupting your work schedule isn't any picnic either. Eventually, all that stress can build up and bleed into every element of your life. An argument with your kid or your spouse can ruin your workday. A bad meeting can lead to snapping at someone at home. It can create a nasty cycle of bad days as the stress and its consequences snowball until there's an avalanche that covers your whole life.

When stress becomes overwhelming enough, it will come out—either in the family, in the office, or in your health. For me, it was a slammed door and back pain. For you, it might be yelling at an employee or punishing your child for a minor mistake.

Allowing this to continue long-term can create a toxic office and a toxic home life in which everyone is trying to read when you're in a bad mood and when you're about to snap. I'm sure that's not the kind of environment you want for your employees or your family. And that means, you've got to start making changes now.

DE-STRESS YOUR OFFICE

Recently, I had a client who threw me under the bus in front of his entire executive team. I was extremely upset, but part of me wanted to just push ahead with the rest of the workday. Instead, I walked back into the office and told my team to cancel the rest of my appointments for the day. I knew I was too stressed, and I wouldn't be emotionally prepared for another meeting.

With a couple hours to myself, I went for a walk. And that's all I did. I didn't check email or make calls. I didn't rush back to fill in some paperwork. I simply took some time to walk away and calm down.

Creating such space for yourself is a crucial part of your journey to becoming a better father and a better entrepreneur. You will have bad days, and finding a way to decompress is valuable for your work in the office and at home. You can't be the best boss for your team if you are so tense you can't think straight. And you can't be a supportive, understanding, energetic father if you're constantly overwhelmed.

That's why I also instituted a "no bad news" policy at my office. On a regular day, unless the situation is truly urgent, I don't let my team bring me bad news before 2 p.m. If I have meetings all afternoon, the bad news has to wait until the next day. Generally, I trust my team to handle the bad news themselves. That way, I can continue to concentrate on maximizing my productivity.

I also set limits on what work can follow me home. While I'll make calls to and from work in the car (Unless my family is with me!), I leave work behind once I pull in. It would take a real crisis to force me to work during that family time in the evening.

That doesn't eliminate all my work stress, but it does allow me to put it aside for the evening so I can spend my energy thinking about the people I love most.

CUT THE TECHNOLOGY LINK

One way to really sever the stress between work and home is to physically leave it behind. And the best way to do that is to cut communication to the office once you get home.

We've become so attached to our technology, it can be almost impossible to turn off our work brains when we're supposed to be enjoying our lives. You answer every call that comes in. You check your email every ten minutes. There are push alerts for everything. You're following every problem, big and small, every update, big and small, throughout your evening and weekends.

That's putting immense stress on your brain. So turn it off. At my company, everyone is given a new phone specifically for work. Their personal phone is their "life" phone. The "life" phone can come to the office, but the work phone shouldn't enter your house.

You can institute a similar policy. Leave that work phone at the office or in the car. Or, if you only have one phone, turn off the push alerts and the ringer. Stop checking email. Create as many barriers between using that technology for work while at home as you can. And when you're taking time for yourself or your family, leave technology out of it.

It's fine to listen to music or a podcast while you're working out or cooking dinner, but don't try to cram more work in even if technology technically makes it possible.

DE-STRESS LIFE TIPS

Even if you can completely separate work stress from the rest of your life, that still leaves the stress you experience at home. While reducing work stress will help handle it, it won't be enough. You need ways to reduce all the stress that's affecting your life. And the best way to do that is to double down on that self-care.

Self-care can take all sorts of forms. In the first place, though, you should attend to your physical and mental health. Make sure you're getting enough sleep. Get up, move around, and exercise as much as you can. In those free moments you can wrestle away for yourself, work on relaxing. You can pray, if that is important to you, or meditate. You can take a few deep breaths or put some music on that calms you.

Beyond fulfilling these basic needs, you should seek out activities that you enjoy. I like hunting, fishing, and being out in nature, but maybe you would prefer golfing, wood working, or going to the movies or painting.

Finally, strengthen the supportive relationships in your life. Spend time with friends or your church or a men's group. Friends are critically important at all stages of our lives, but perhaps never more so than when we have so much responsibility. But make sure these are supportive relationships where you will be encouraged to make positive choices in your life. Having some people in your life who can understand and support you can help you reduce stress and refocus on what matters most, but only if they're helping you achieve that balance you're aiming for.

Seeking friendship is no excuse to go out and get drunk with your buddies every Friday night. It's good to blow off steam but try to do it in a constructive way. You don't want your kids to see you as a man who is always either working or drinking with his friends.

Instead, find positive ways to recharge. Seek out activities that both reduce stress and create opportunities to share your struggles—situations in which you feel comfortable being vulnerable and open. That is not always easy for men. Many male friendships are built on some sort of masculine competitiveness, and while that's fine if that competitiveness is enjoyable to you—perhaps you unwind by playing pick-up basketball—you still need to look for a network that allows you to talk about family and work in a real and emotionally honest way.

LET YOUR FAMILY IN

Making these life changes are important, but that doesn't mean you always have to seek assistance with your stress outside the family. You don't have to be the traditional stoic dad who never shares what he's thinking or feeling. You can let some of your stress out by talking about a difficult day at the office over dinner. You should be able to look forward to a hug and some comfort from your kids, and you have a right to expect understanding from your spouse.

That's not a license to force your family into becoming a team of therapists for you, but when things are tough it's always better to communicate that you are struggling than to try to hide it. Communication can explain to your family why you've been short with them or why you might need a little extra time for yourself. It's far better to clarify this than to leave your family guessing and filling in explanations for themselves.

That stoic dad isn't actually decreasing stress in the family. He's adding to it. Instead of knowing how Dad is feeling and what he needs from his family and for himself, everyone will be on edge when you come home. Is Dad quiet because he's tired or because he's had a bad day? Does that mean he's upset? Is he upset with the family? Is he going to yell?

All of that can be defused if you create an environment in which everyone can be honest about the difficulties they're facing, and the family can do whatever possible to reduce that stress.

IS THIS STRESS WORTH IT?

You can make all of these adjustments and still find that, sometimes, you're still stressed and unhappy. It would be disingenuous of me to suggest such periods are entirely avoidable. After all, for all my prayers, things were still difficult in my household for a good while. When Brooke switched veterinarian clinics, she started working weekends, and that stress eventually led to the moment we actually contemplated divorce.

Stress is inevitable in life. In such moments, it's good to return to your *whys* and think hard about whether this is really the life you want. Starting and running a business is extremely difficult and comes with a heavy set of responsibilities. Is this definitely the path you still want to be on? Is it worth the struggles you are facing?

I left behind one successful business for another precisely because it wasn't worth that stress to me. Brooke switched clinics for the same reason. There's no shame in taking a new path if the one you are on currently is making you miserable. It is okay to walk away from entrepreneurship—forever or just for a time—if you and your family would be happier if you had a corporate job. It's also okay to forgo climbing that corporate ladder if you don't actually want to reach the next rung.

I recently met with a couple clients. They're retired dentists in their early seventies, and they did very well in life—with almost $5 million in their portfolio. In addition to the retirement funds, they have a beautiful home with forty acres, two condos, and a place on the lake.

For the last two years, though, all I've heard from them is how miserable they are because of all the work they have to do to keep all those properties up. As they launched into another dispute right in front of me—hoping for me to be the tiebreaker between them—I pulled them up short.

"Most people have only one house," I told them. "You have four. Are those houses making you happy? Do you really get a lot out of all that property? Is this how you want the rest of your life to be—filled with arguments about keeping up a bunch of homes you rarely visit?"

The truth is, they had all that property because they thought that's what successful people do. Other successful people have a house and a place on the lake. To prove they really hit the top, they wanted the house and the place on the lake plus two condos. But that choice was adding a lot of stress they didn't need in their lives. It was hurting what mattered—their relationship—for what didn't.

And they'd be better off simply selling the extra property and enjoying the time they have together.

LESS STRESS IMPROVES YOUR TIME WITH FAMILY

Recently, my son, Bryce, came home with a business idea. He wants to start a specialty manufacturing business. Brooke and I are considering providing the seed money. We'd also help him run the business side of things while he does the work.

But there's a catch. To help run his business, I'd have to step further away from my own. I almost certainly would lose money on that deal. It's unlikely his new company could pay me as much as mine does. But I'm still considering doing it. I'm blessed to be in a position in which that extra income isn't necessary for any of my needs or even my wants. And what I'd earn instead is far more important: a chance to be a part of what my son loves doing. I could be the one who makes his dream happen.

In my opinion, nothing could be more rewarding than that. Undoubtedly, founding a new company would be stressful, but I think it's the kind of stress worth taking on because it would allow me to be close to Bryce and to show him just how much I believe in him. And taking an interest in what he finds interesting is perhaps the best way to strengthen our connection.

Chapter 8

TAKE AN INTEREST

As a man whose life revolved around athletics, you would think that my father would have easily connected to my brother, Scott, and me when we turned out to share an interest in sports. Scott, in particular, was relatively accomplished in various athletic pursuits. He ran cross country and was a very good basketball player throughout high school. My own athletic career ended after a severe knee injury I suffered playing football my freshman year.

For all our efforts, though, Dad remained far more focused on the athletic activities occurring at his school. He would show up to watch Scott when he could, but it wasn't that often. And he drove me to the doctor for rehab—partly because my mother was livid that I'd been hurt playing contact sports—and encouraged me to get back to sports once I was healed.

But when it became clear that I wouldn't ever be able to play competitive sports again, he drifted away again. I don't really remember him being there to comfort me or help me find a new direction. He simply didn't know how to build a connection.

This was the story of Scott and my youth. Dad was too busy and aloof to ever take an extended interest. But things changed a decade later after Dad retired. Once he finally had more time, he wanted to make up for his mistakes. Suddenly, in my early thirties, Dad wanted *my* attention. He wanted to spend time with me and share my interests. Unfortunately, by then it was too late. I was a young man with my own life, and I couldn't make much room for him. Much like the song "Cat's in the Cradle," the need of the son had turned into the need of the father and led to a new disappointment.

It was even worse with Scott, who had lived with my dad throughout his childhood and had tried so hard to get his attention. Scott could never forgive my dad for those lonely, disappointed years. While I tried to make some accommodation for Dad's new interest, Scott shut the door on him almost entirely.

Those relationships were never repaired. After he died, Scott and I went through Dad's possessions. Amongst the various items he'd held onto, we found not records of our own athletic achievements but a number of plaques his school had given him to celebrate his commitment to his students.

They all read something like, "Thank you for all the time you put into the kids."

Far from feeling pride for his dedication or any positive association from our childhood, we found that these plaques simply reminded us of his absence—his disinterest, even if he never meant it to come across that way.

After we held a service and spread his ashes, we ended up burning the plaques in a bonfire. They didn't mean anything to us beyond the pain.

SHARE IN THE PASSION

I'm sure you don't want your children to feel that way about you when you pass. That's why you're here. Using the advice we've covered so far, you can go a long way to avoiding that future, but there's still far more to do. And one area where you can start is by building more robust ties to your children by taking an interest in what interests them.

Simply put, you have to be passionate about their passions, even when those interests don't align with yours. These interests may require you to stretch yourself significantly and find a way into activities that fall far outside your own comfort zone.

That's certainly been the case with both of my children. I am not very mechanical, but Bryce proved to be just that from a very early age. At four, he became obsessed with going straight from his tricycle straight to a bicycle without ever using training wheels. From that first successful ride in a big open lot (free of objects he could run into) to today, he's always been interested in anything with wheels.

After the bicycle, it was scooters. Once he'd mastered that, he wanted to start visiting the skatepark where he could try to emulate the tricks the older kids were doing. At thirteen, he wanted a unicycle so badly that he tried to cut up an old bike and make one himself. When we bought him a real unicycle, he practiced on it so much that he eventually rode it all the way up a mountain.

His other major interest was putting things together. Early on, he became passionate about Legos—again, something that went very against my own strengths. I have ADHD, and I cannot sit down and put little bricks together for hours. I'm simply incapable of it. But Bryce loved that more than almost anything. We still get him a new set of Legos every Christmas.

It was no easier with Morgan, whose interests were vastly different but still didn't overlap with mine. For Morgan, it was animals. She loved animals from a very young age, particularly horses. She's always enjoyed being close to horses and interacting with them. We got her into a program that showed her how to safely be around them and develop a relationship with them before she began her riding lessons. Eventually, we leased a horse for her so she could perform in dressage.

These interests have carried through the entire young lives of both my kids. Until recently, Bryce was one of the lead mechanics for the racecar development team, Road to Indy. Morgan is studying to be a veterinarian.

And I would have missed out on some of the most important parts of their lives if I hadn't been there to support them, urge them along, and share in their passion—even when it wasn't my natural interest.

DON'T JUST ASK, PARTICIPATE

Supporting those passions goes beyond simply acknowledging them or providing a little positive enforcement.

With your busy life and lack of extra energy, it might feel like enough to ask regularly about your children's hobbies and interests and listen as attentively as possible. That's a great start, but if you really want to be a part of their lives, you should participate in those interests as much as you can.

For instance, with Bryce, despite the fact I'm not a tinkerer like him, I still spent hundreds of hours playing around with junk engines that we purchased from the scrapyard. When he struggled in regular college, I took the time to help him find a high-performance automotive school that put him on track to work with engines and race cars for the rest of his life. Then his mom and I helped him apply for admission.

For Morgan, I leased that horse and then took horse riding lessons with her. I also went to as many of her horse shows as I could—despite the fact they often consisted of excruciatingly long waits to see her show her horse for fifteen minutes.

Of course, this was not all about me. Brooke and I tried to divide our time evenly and switch events so that we were able to participate equally. If I was at a horse show, Brooke was at the skatepark or a lacrosse match for Bryce. The next weekend, we'd switch places.

Beyond that, we tried to split the practical parts of participation into the areas where we were strongest. As a vet, it made sense for Brooke to take on the medical care for Morgan's horse, including the shoeing and vaccinations. She also did most of the play with Legos because she has a natural interest in carefully putting those projects together. When it came to horse riding or engine building, though, that was on me.

We both found these elements within our children's interests that spoke most to us, so that we could enjoy participating as much as possible.

SHARE WHAT YOU LOVE

Your children's interests are important, and you should connect with them through those passions—but that doesn't mean you can't share what you love with them, so long as you're careful about how you do it.

In the first place, don't try to force them to love what you love or to love it in the way you do. I've seen plenty of fathers become extremely frustrated because their children didn't take to hunting or sports or some other activity the way Dad might have hoped. But that frustration only drives children further away from those interests.

Instead, introduce what you care about in a way that allows your children to accept it on their own terms. For instance, I've always made it a priority to share my love of nature with my kids. From a very early age, I put Bryce in a little baby pack and went out for nature walks and fishing trips with him next to me. When Morgan arrived, I did the same thing all over again.

But as they got old enough to participate in my interests, I made sure to adapt those activities to make nature interesting for children. I bought Bryce a Batman fishing pole from Walmart, and I would take him fishing at ponds with a lot of small fish that he could catch before getting bored. We'd cast only as long as the fish were biting. I can still remember when he caught this tiny little fish for the first time. He was ecstatic.

When he grew older, we would do target shooting and shoot pop cans because he found that to be more fun than hours out in the woods hunting. I spent tons of time building big campfires and roasting hot dogs, playing chaperon so the kids could run around with their friends outdoors, and looking for crawfish—because that allowed my children to love nature in their own way.

Whatever the activity, I always made sure both kids had warm clothes and the weather was good, so that we had the optimal chance for a good day.

My friend Jess has had a similar experience. When he started taking his son Kolby out fishing, Kolby found it a bit boring. What he liked, though, was chasing frogs, playing in the mud, and skipping stones. These days, the kid is as passionate about the outdoors as his father. And Bryce and Morgan love to go camping. We still go out and cook up those hot dogs.

They all came to love the same thing Jess and I do because they came to that love on their own. It was their interest—not mine or Jess's.

This can be a hard lesson to learn. So often, parents push a little too hard to get their kids to love and excel in the areas the parents care about. I've seen parents organize the entire family around pushing for one kid to make the Olympic team when it wasn't clear anyone was enjoying it.

If you love sports, that's great. Share that interest. But if your kid wants to play soccer instead of football or would rather watch the game with you than play it, that's fine too. Morgan played soccer, but she played it for the social element. And that was fine because she found her own way to enjoy the game.

The same is true if you love music. Play music for your kids. If they show an interest in one instrument or another, go out and rent one or buy one. But if they grow tired of lessons and don't enjoy it, don't force that love on them. You can take them to concerts for music that you like but don't exclude the concerts they might prefer to go to. Let them come to love music on their terms, and eventually, you'll be able to share that love together.

FIND WAYS TO CONNECT WITH YOUR SPOUSE

What is true for your kids is also true for your spouse. Even with your interests pretty well locked in and habits already formed, it's important to find ways to connect on this level. For some, that may be easy. Perhaps you and your spouse have always shared some interests. If you both love cooking, classic movies, or marathon running, then all you have to do is remember to share that passion together. Take a new cooking class, set a movie night, or get in a few runs each week together.

For others like Brooke and me, though, this isn't so easy. Brooke and I have very different interests. Brooke is extremely creative and artistic. She loves crafting. There's not a ton of overlap between that and my love of nature and hunting.

But that's no excuse to pursue those interests completely separately. In the first place, there's a responsibility to be attentive to what your partner cares about even when you don't share the interest. I know all about the classes Brooke takes and the projects she's working on. I know that she's currently working on improving her sewing skills. The same should hold for your interactions with your spouse, whether their interests are quilts, CrossFit, or acting in amateur stage productions on the weekend. You have to engage in and encourage your spouse's pursuits just as you would your children, whatever your own level of interest.

You should also find opportunities to participate when you can. If your spouse is doing a production of *Oklahoma*, you should be in the audience, even if you hate musicals. Even if it leaves you sore, it wouldn't hurt to try a CrossFit class every once in a while either. For Brooke and me, I attend craft fairs and do my best to understand why she finds them interesting, and she will go to hunting shows for my benefit. Neither of us requires too much time from the other at these events, but it's meaningful all the same.

Beyond that, it's valuable to look for areas in which you can actually combine interests, no matter how different they might be. Brooke and I have stumbled upon the realization that we both really like glass fusing. For her, there's that artistic fulfillment in creating the objects. I enjoy finding ways to create objects that represent the things I love.

Together, we created a glass version of our cabin out in the woods—a way to reflect on nature even during those busy work weeks in town. And when Dad passed, we created a glass-fused ornament to hold some of his ashes. Creating that provided a powerful sense of togetherness when I needed it most.

That hobby has become *our* thing, a thing we can cherish together and that has helped me through difficult times. And that has come to mean a great deal to both of us.

ALLOW FOR SEPARATION AS WELL

I wouldn't trade the time I've spent glass-fusing, horse riding, or engine repairing for anything, even though all of those things fall well outside my own natural interests. However, that doesn't mean I would do these things all the time. In fact, though connection is important, it's also important to allow each member of your family to explore their interests independently sometimes—and that includes pursuing your own interests as well. Like everything, it's about balance.

While Brooke and I share glass fusing and I ask about her crafts, she does most of that work on her own. And Bryce has entire hobbies I barely interact with at all. He loves video games, and I just don't play much of a part in that. If he's home and puts a game on in the living room, I'll sit down and watch him wander around those digital worlds. I'll ask if he has any new games he's particularly enjoying. Beyond that, though, it's something that belongs to him.

It's something that's his—and it's good that it's his.

No one in your family should feel obligated to share every part of their life with you. People need their own space and a chance to be separate and independent. Providing that space only helps strengthen your relationship. Otherwise, your interest can become smothering.

You certainly don't want your spouse feeling that they can't ever get time to themselves or leave your children feeling they need Dad to hold their hand through every activity they ever take up.

If your child doesn't want you to watch their garage band practice every week, that's fine. It's good, even. You want them to have an independent life.

That's not an easy balance to strike, but it's an important one. And it's certainly not the only balancing act you'll have to perform, either. Because it's even more important that you find the right balance between providing support and discipline—whether your kids are still your little angels, or they've turned into teenage monsters.

CHAPTER 9

LOVE AND RESPECT

THESE DAYS, MY KIDS AND I ARE BEST FRIENDS, BUT IT hasn't always been that way. In fact, their teenage years were as difficult as you could imagine.

With Bryce, it was largely his academic performance. He is very intelligent, but he really struggled in high school. My response to this was not my finest moment. I was often too hard on him, and that reaction probably pushed him to be more rebellious than he might otherwise have been. We were worried he was on drugs (thankfully that was unfounded), and I think it insulted him that we didn't trust him. At one point, he took our pickup truck—without a driver's license—and drove off with the intention of running away.

Amazingly, things with Morgan were even tougher. When she turned thirteen, I began to wonder if someone had kidnapped my daughter and replaced her with an extremely disagreeable look-alike. Seemingly overnight, she became moody, demanding, and difficult. She refused to do anything productive and constantly complained. She slammed her door so much, I had to take it off its hinges. At one point, we even had to go with the old-school washing her mouth out with soap.

These were incredibly difficult years. I don't know how my family got through them.

Actually, I do. It came down to a few key choices. Brooke and I broke from the tradition of strict disciplinarianism and still managed to set rules, stand by those rules, and show love throughout. In the end, that was enough to get through the hard times and bring us closer once they were over.

BREAK THE OLD RULES

Brooke and I started at a real disadvantage in the parental department. We had very little training in how to effectively discipline kids or show them affection. Brooke's father had a "children should be seen and not heard, and preferably not seen" mentality. My father was largely absent and struggled to share his emotions.

The easiest path would have been to follow those examples or else to default to the traditional standard expectation set for parents: strict disciplinarian Dad and permissive Mom. When there aren't better examples available, many men still fall into the role of the father who comes home, yells at the kids (or the spouse) for not following one rule or another, and hands out punishments.

In that traditional role, Dad spends all of his energy on work and comes home with an expectation that everything is taken care of so he can relax. Dinner should be cooked, the TV should be ready for him, and he should be left alone. The limited interaction that he has with his family is through enforcement of rules—often arbitrary and based on his comfort. Enforcement comes down to shouting and punishing.

Entrepreneurs are unfortunately quite susceptible to following this pattern. They are often out of the home most of the time. Their work is extremely energy-intensive, leaving them exhausted when they do get home. And if they aren't careful, their interactions in the evening amount to demanding perfect behavior from everyone in the household.

But there's a cost to that kind of parenting. Your kids can become afraid of you. While by nature they may look forward to the moment you walk in the door, eventually, they'll come to hear that garage door opening with a sense of dread. What will Dad yell about tonight?

Working on your schedule and your stress can help avoid that future, but you also need to establish a better way to guide your children and partner with your spouse. That's the key to helping your kids become the best people they can be while also providing the assistance your partner needs.

DON'T BE TOO LENIENT

You don't want to be that grouchy disciplinarian dad whose kids are afraid of him, but in trying to avoid that role it's easy to overcorrect. From the tyrannical Dad demanding to be left alone in front of the TV, you can become too easy-going, too permissive, and too willing to let your children get away with anything.

I've seen this before. A friend of mine has a daughter who is now in her twenties. When she was younger, he essentially refused to discipline her. That meant no rules and no enforcement. If Mom wanted her to behave a certain way, she would have to handle that side of parenting alone. He had a distant relationship with his own parents, and he wanted to make sure his daughter felt like she had a friend in him.

But as his daughter reached her teenage years, this strategy led to some very significant problems. His daughter began to spiral out of control. She was attending parties with alcohol and older men. She became promiscuous. My friend and his daughter were extremely lucky that there were no serious consequences for that behavior.

To be so relaxed about discipline is an abandonment of one of your chief roles as a father: to help your child grow up with the morals and ethics they need to stay safe and succeed in life. To instill those morals and ethics requires doing the unfun stuff like setting rules and enforcing them—as a team with your spouse—and accepting that sometimes you won't be your child's best friend.

That's not to say there's nothing wrong with wanting to be friends with your kids, but you have to be a father first. That means you aren't just the fun pal who lets them get away with anything and have everything they want. You have to be the best friend they ever have, the one who calls out their bad behavior, tells them what they need to hear, and helps them to be the best person they can be.

In my men's group, we use a biblical expression to capture that need for tough honesty in relationships: "iron sharpens iron." This isn't just true for strong male friendships, it's also true of fatherhood. You have to be that iron for your children. That's how you help them become as tough as iron themselves. It's also how you show them that they can trust you and rely on you to take care of them. And that's central to building any friendship.

SET RULES

If you aren't going to be a strict disciplinarian or let the kids run wild, how do you provide structure and hit that balance between love, friendship, and authority?

You start by setting the rules. Having rules is important for kids. They crave structure because it gives them a sense of their place in the world. If they know what they are permitted to do, what is expected of them, and where they are allowed to show independence and make their own decisions, they feel safer and more comfortable.

Your household rules should fit your own view of proper behavior, and you should set them with your spouse as early as possible. Rules should be carefully considered, agreed upon by both parents, and updated as necessary. These rules will provide the boundaries of what is acceptable for your children. They will push against those boundaries—that's how kids are—but they will also understand better why they are being held accountable.

In my house, we had a mix of obvious rules and some that were a bit unique. There was a rule that we would always have dinner all together, and one that everyone had to help clean up the dishes afterward. We had a rule to limit TV—only after homework. We had plenty of hygiene rules, including a bath or shower every day (which Bryce at one point rebelled against), brushing teeth, and keeping family spaces cleaned up. That last one was particularly difficult for Morgan, who by nature tends to leave a room a little messier than she found it.

In addition, there was a curfew of 9 p.m. If one of the kids was going to be later than that, they had to call, and there was no excuse for regularly missing curfew.

I also set a rule about the quality of their chores. If Bryce or Morgan was mowing the lawn, I expected it to be well-mown. If they were washing the dishes, those dishes should pass a cleanliness inspection. If they clearly rushed the work, they were expected to do it all over again.

None of these rules were designed to be particularly oppressive or demanding—although the kids certainly made those complaints—and we allowed some leniency from time to time, but for the most part, we stood firm. The kids knew what was expected of them, and if they fell short, they knew they could expect consequences.

FOLLOW THROUGH WITH CONSEQUENCES

Whatever your rules, your kids are going to hate them. They need them, but they will hate them—and they will break them. When that happens, you have to be prepared to lay down consequences. If there are no consequences, kids never really see these boundaries are rules. They, quite rightly, recognize that there is no real boundary there at all. Rules then become less a structure to the family than a set of obstacles they have to find their way around.

Handing down consequences is no fun. Morgan's struggles with sloppiness have led to her being late to horse events—and you can be sure she made it very clear just how little she appreciated that. There have been times when we've had to hire a babysitter to watch one or both kids because they broke a rule, so they could remain home while the rest of the family went off to enjoy an afternoon. We even had to invoke this punishment on vacation in Hawaii. We were out on the islands during Morgan's fourteenth birthday. Instead of being cheerful, though, her behavior was awful. We ended up having to leave her behind in the condo we were renting for an entire day because she was ruining the trip for everyone.

Trust me, you don't have to lay down such heavy punishments often before your kids learn exactly how far they can push things. It's unpleasant at the time, but it makes an impact.

COMMUNICATE WITH LOVE

In those difficult moments when you're laying down the law with your child, you probably want it over with as quickly as possible. You're upset, they're upset, and you want them in their room or cleaning the bathroom or whatever they have to do—whatever it takes to conclude this unpleasant moment—immediately.

However, it's extremely important to take a breath in such moments and explain yourself. As I've mentioned several times already, communication is critical in strong family relationships. Your kids need to know why you're doing this and what you want them to get out of this punishment.

"I'm taking away the PlayStation because you failed to turn in your homework for the third time this month. Hopefully now you'll remember to focus on your studies before you spend the rest of the evening gaming."

"I'm grounding you for the weekend because you yelled at your mother. She deserves your respect. Next time, let's find a better way to communicate how we're upset."

This may do little to defuse the situation in that moment, but explaining why a punishment is happening helps your kid understand that you aren't doing this just because you're a power-hungry patriarchal tyrant who likes to see them suffer. There's a reason behind this, and you have their best interests at heart—even if they feel you're overreacting.

Whether during this little speech or shortly afterward, you also want to make it clear to them that you love them. If you've done a good job so far, they know that you love them on some level, but it's easy to lose sight of that in difficult times. My own children would often throw this sort of accusation at me. In their teenage years, I'd regularly hear the same refrain: "I hate you, and I know you don't love me."

And Brooke and I always responded the same way: "Nice try. You are correct that we don't like you much right now. But we do love you."

They'll protest or shrug or roll their eyes sometimes, but they need to know that, even if they think you're impossible and lame and a real pain in the butt, that you are making their lives tough because you love them. And you will love them through any misbehavior or mistake they ever make.

Reminding your children that you love them even when they are impossible to live with is so critical because there will come a time when they truly need you. Maybe it's a hug after their first breakup. Maybe it's compassion after their first fender bender. Or maybe it's support after something much bigger goes wrong. But at some point, they'll need your love and understanding, and you want them to know that you are ready to prove it.

In any of those scenarios, you want their instinct to be that they can come to you. If you're always a disciplinarian and you never make it explicitly clear why they've been punished or that you love them unconditionally, they may try to hide their screw-ups or emotional heartache from you. If you let them get away with everything, they may think you aren't reliable when things get tough.

That's why you've got to get the balance right. Because you definitely want to be the one offering that hug when it's required.

DON'T GIVE UP

For this system to work best, you have to set these rules and make them clear long before your kids reach the age at which they really start rebelling (usually in their teens). It's very difficult to start putting limits on your children when they're fourteen and accustomed to having their own way about everything. Discipline is always painful—but trying to impose rules at that point will be even more so.

But it's not impossible. If you're trying to create stability and structure in the midst of childhood rebellion, you can take some difficult but very concrete steps towards making this situation better. Start by communicating with your spouse. When possible, you need to set new rules together. You should also strengthen your support network. Open up lines of communication with those who are going through this or have already been through this. That gives you an outlet for your own frustrations and also an avenue to gain some extra advice. Then you have to stand by the new rules, even when it is extremely difficult.

And whatever you do, don't give up.

Whether you're building a family dynamic of love and respect while your kids are young or trying to scrape it together when they are in their teens, you will almost certainly make mistakes. You'll come down too hard some-times. At other times, you'll find you've been too lenient. You'll get grouchy and forget to explain yourself or push your kids away as if you were one of those "kids should be seen not heard" dads from a generation ago.

That is inevitable. But the biggest difference you can make for your children is to keep trying. That's how you really show love and commitment, and that's how you get as close as humanly possible to finding that balance.

Chapter 10

IT'S OKAY TO MAKE MISTAKES

Back when Bryce was in kindergarten, his teacher came up to us and told us that he had a hearing issue. She recommended that we get him tested. Being the attentive parents we are, Brooke and I immediately signed him up for a test at the school and then took him to see a doctor. But nothing came up. According to the test results, Bryce's hearing was nearly perfect.

But the issue wouldn't go away. Every couple of years, another teacher would tell us the same thing. There was some trouble with his hearing, and we should get him checked. We continued to get him tested—we even took him to a Washington State University hearing clinic—but the results never changed.

Things got worse when Bryce hit middle school. Until that point, he'd always done well in school, but suddenly, he started failing classes. Just as worrying, he refused to take any responsibility for his plummeting grades. Instead, he blamed his teachers, telling us that they were giving him confusing instructions—making it impossible for him to finish the work. His teachers, for their part, insisted this wasn't the case.

We spent thousands of dollars trying to address this mysterious change. We sent Bryce to therapy and organization management courses. We did everything we could think of. He kept struggling.

The only reasonable option left, as far as Brooke and I could tell, was to assume Bryce was choosing to fail. As such, we were extremely tough on him. We accused him of being on drugs. We would ground him for whole weekends. We continually pressed him and pushed him to improve. We were frustrated, and we let him know it.

That only made him act out more and turn against us.

In our desperation, we went to a psychologist, who once again recommended we get Bryce's hearing tested. I pointed out in exasperation that we had been doing hearing tests for a decade at that point, and nothing ever came up. Perhaps, the psychologist told us, that wasn't because there was no issue but because we were running the wrong tests.

Following his advice, we went to a clinic in Spokane and asked them to run further tests. The first test was the standard hearing test Bryce had been taking for years. He aced it as he always did, landing in the top 90 percent of hearers. The second test was new to us. In that test, they introduced background noise that slightly interfered with the sound Bryce was listening for.

That's when we got our answer. That second test told us that Bryce was in the fourth percentile for processing what he was hearing when background noise was introduced. Essentially, his brain confused the various sounds he was hearing. In a classroom, if the teacher was talking, some kids were whispering behind him, and a car was driving by outside, his brain put all those sounds together. That was why he felt he was getting confusing instructions.

This was the first we had ever heard of auditory processing, and the diagnosis explained so much. We'd often been frustrated by Bryce seemingly purposefully misunderstanding basic instructions. If we told him it was time to eat, odds were we'd find him in the bathtub ten minutes later, claiming we had demanded he clean his feet.

This was undeniably great news. We had an answer, and there were treatment options. But I was devastated—not because Bryce had an auditory issue. It was because I'd been so hard on him. He had done nothing wrong for all those years, and I hadn't been there for him the way he needed me to be. He had told me the truth, and I'd accused him of drug use and purposefully misbehaving. He had needed my support, and I'd grounded him.

I'd made one of the worst mistakes of my life, and I could never undo it.

NO ONE IS PERFECT

If I've given the impression that I am a perfect father in this book, I hope that story proves the opposite. Like everyone, I have made my share of mistakes, big and small. Like you, I can't turn stress off like a light switch. There are days when I come home, and I don't manage to pray that stress away. I snap at people when I shouldn't and say things I regret.

Even today with my kids grown and my work responsibility well-managed, there are days I come home grouchy or tired, and I don't want to spend that quality time with anyone. Brooke is the same way. Some days, we just don't have energy for that connection.

For as important as those Thursday lunches are, Brooke and I have missed two of them this month. Bryce is home for a bit, and there's a holiday meal to prepare for, and those lunches got away from us. We managed to put together a nice dinner alone, but it took a lot of extra effort to fit it in.

I managed to instill a set of rules and responsibilities in my kids, but I didn't always get the balance right. I probably should have pushed Morgan to clean up her own room more instead of letting that go. And I clearly missed the mark with Bryce's hearing difficulties.

In every part of fatherhood and marriage, I've failed at times. And I expect to continue to fail for the rest of my life.

ACCEPT THAT YOU AREN'T ALWAYS IN CONTROL

Mistakes are inevitable even when things are going well, but they are particularly common in moments we can't control. I have been very lucky to have a great deal of control over my life. I have been able to set my schedule, build a business, and balance my time without too much disruption. But there were still times when I wasn't in control of my choices. Bryce's hearing issue is an obvious example. I had no way to prevent that difficulty and no way of knowing why it was happening.

This is often the case. I spent a lot of time with my kids when they were growing up, but I still wish we'd had more time. I wish we could have gone fishing and camping more often. At the same time, I wasn't always in control of those choices. There were times when I had to be at work. There was a crisis or an important client with a major request, and I had to put that first. I couldn't control the hours Brooke had to work when she was gone on weekends, which added tension to our relationship. I couldn't control Morgan's change in personality when she was a teen.

For you, that lack of control may show up on a financial level. Perhaps your business isn't growing as you expected, and money has been tight. Perhaps there's a sudden illness or a case of burnout. These issues will come up, and all you can do is to do your best, adapt as much as possible, and give yourself a break. You're doing your best as an entrepreneur and a father. When things are beyond your control, you have no choice but to muddle through and then learn whatever lessons you can to reduce the chance that issue comes up again.

LEARN FROM YOUR MISTAKES

The fact that you can't control life and that you will make mistakes is always unwelcome news to entrepreneurs.

Entrepreneurs are often extremely driven perfectionists who want to get everything right. But as a father and a business owner, you are going to have to come to terms with your limitations—and then seek to improve as you go along.

And that requires recognizing your mistakes when you make them and learning from them.

This is a difficult skill. Often, pride and intense emotion get in the way of both recognition and learning. When Brooke and I were struggling, and I snapped at the family before slamming the door, it wasn't easy to open myself up to self-criticism. I was ashamed and embarrassed of how I had responded. At the same time, I was angry at Brooke, my children, and myself. It was hard to work through all of those emotions to see the lessons I needed to learn. It would have been far easier in that moment to try to blame the others involved. I could have blamed Brooke for her weekend work schedule or for not keeping the kids in line. I could have blamed the kids for not behaving better.

But blaming everyone else wasn't going to help my family or improve things. If I wanted to keep my family together, I had to put my initial reactions aside and learn the necessary lessons to pull us back from the brink.

To remove the emotion from those circumstances, I introduced an entrepreneurial system into my self-reflections on my work as a father and a husband: plan, do, review. That's how I came up with my "pray before entering" idea. I planned what I could do the next time I was that stressed and I came home to an upset house. I put that plan in place, and afterward, I reviewed my progress. That doesn't mean I always held my tongue and perfectly deescalated the emotions in the house, but I did *better*. And *better* is the key to finding balance in your work as a dad and as an entrepreneur.

KEEP TRYING

Back when Bryce was struggling, someone in my men's group introduced us to a program called "Letters from Dad." I loved the idea, and I jumped right into it. I even taught a workshop on the topic. In that workshop, each father wrote letters to his kids and spouses about everything that he appreciated about each of them. The rule was that there could be no criticism. This was a letter of pure love and support. It had to be filled with recognition of the things that made a child unique and the things that the father loved about that child.

I wrote my letter to Bryce. It wasn't easy. I think of myself as an emotionally open man, but I still struggled to get those words down on the page. By the end, there were a lot of tears all over that letter. It was extremely heartfelt and sincere. It was a labor of love.

More than that—though I didn't know it at the time—that letter would save my son's life. After he received it, Bryce put that letter in a lockbox. A couple years later, he told his psychologist that in those tough times, he'd considered killing himself. The combination of his struggles at school and the lack of support at home had left him feeling that he simply wasn't good enough.

That letter played a central role in keeping him going. That one letter, that one act of fatherly love, helped my boy get through the toughest moment of his life. There was so much I was getting wrong in that period—but getting that one thing right made the difference.

That's why fathers have to keep trying. Whether you are just starting out in fatherhood and entrepreneurship or you're more than a decade in and a decade behind where you wanted to be, the single most important thing you can do is to keep putting in that effort to do a little better.

With Bryce, continuing to do a little better meant redoubling my support after we got his diagnosis. It meant encouraging him to wear his hearing aid even though he was a moody insecure teenager who didn't want to stand out. It meant moving him to an alternative high school when it was clear he wasn't comfortable staying where he was.

By constantly putting that effort in, Bryce knew, when he got a little older, that he could come to me when he was ready to start wearing that hearing aid. In fact, I was the person he asked to take him shopping for one when he was nineteen. Despite my screw-ups, he trusted, respected, and loved me.

You can arrive at that place too, so long as you commit to doing a little better tomorrow than you are doing today. As Dan Sullivan's Strategic Coach program puts it to entrepreneurs: "it's progress not perfection."

That's the advice I gave a friend of mine who is expecting his first child with his wife. He's working too many hours, and he freely admits that right now, all his wife gets are the scraps of energy and attention he can spare at the end of the day.

I told him the same thing I am telling you: tomorrow is the first day of the rest of your life. If you want to be a better husband, a better father, and a better kind of entrepreneur, take that tomorrow and live life better. Find a little more time for what matters, put a little more attention on why you're trying to take on so much, try a new strategy to decrease a little stress, take a little more interest in the interests of someone you love, stick a little closer to these rules and tell someone you love them, or learn a little more from a past mistake.

Just do a little better. That's the first step on the way to getting the family-business balancing act right.

My whole family, with Bryce and Morgan all grown up.

CONCLUSION

IT'S CLICHÉ, BUT IT'S TRUE: IF YOU WANT TO DO IT RIGHT, family is going to be the hardest thing you ever take on. To be the father and husband you want to be, you are going to have to start making some major changes, and that in and of itself is quite hard. Making and breaking mindsets and habits requires a lot of dedication.

There's a lot of work ahead, so the best thing you can do for yourself, your business, and your family is to start implementing the ideas in this book today. Don't let a day pass before you begin reorganizing your office to provide you extra time and opening spaces in your schedule for family. Don't wait to reduce your stress, take part in family interests, or set family rules.

As you start making these changes, look out for the "guys" who might push you toward the wrong choices for you and your family. And if you look in the mirror and see a workaholic, a corporate taskmaster, an obsessive credentialist, or someone who puts fancy cars ahead of family, that's all the more reason to make changing a serious priority.

There is no time to delay. Life is full of unexpected events, and if you don't begin to put these ideas to work right away, the unexpected will take over.

If you're still struggling to get started, you can engrain these ideas by placing reminders for yourself. You might consider setting an alarm to go off at the same time each week to check your progress on the various steps you're taking. I met a presenter at a Strategic Coach session who wears a bracelet to remind himself to make the effort to be a better grandpa every single day.

You can also increase your motivation by sharing these ideas with others. Call a few friends who are in similar circumstances and suggest you all pursue these ideas together and hold one another accountable. You might seek out others who are particularly struggling to balance fatherhood and entrepreneurship and try to mentor them to be the dad they want to be.

If you need more guidance on the hows, whats, and whys of balancing family and business, I've included a list of suggested reading after the conclusion. For further personal guidance, I'm always available for coaching, and I will happily speak to groups if you'd like to spread this message further. For any of those needs, you can reach out to me at Progress Not Perfection Strategies, pnpstrategies@outlook.com.

However you pursue the advice in this book, though, pursue it now. This is a journey of progress, and you want to start that journey as soon as possible. Childhood doesn't last forever, and every day you put this off is a little extra distance you have to make up to create that relationship you want with your kids. You may only take one step each day, but that is one step in the direction you want to be heading—toward a world in which you are the entrepreneur and family man you always intended to be.

FURTHER READING

Do Life Differently: A Strategic Path toward Extraordinary by Jeff D. Reeter

The Gap and The Gain: The High Achievers' Guide to Happiness, Confidence, and Success by Dan Sullivan and Dr. Benjamin Hardy

Letters From Dad: How to Leave a Legacy of Faith, Hope, and Love for Your Family by Greg Vaughn

"The Power of Vulnerability. Teachings of Authenticity, Connection, and Courage," TED Talk by Brené Brown

Rising Strong: How the Ability to Reset Transforms the Way We Live, Love, Parent, and Lead by Brené Brown

Start with Why: How Great Leaders Inspire Everyone to Take Action by Simon Sinek

Who Not How: The Formula to Achieve Bigger Goals Through Accelerating Teamwork by Dan Sullivan and Dr. Benjamin Hardy

Your Life by Design: A Step-by-Step Guide to Creating a Bigger Future by Curtis R. Estes

ACKNOWLEDGMENTS

SO MANY PEOPLE HAVE BEEN IMPORTANT IN HELPING ME become a better entrepreneur, a better father, and a better husband. I'd like to thank Dan Sullivan and Babs Smith for creating the Strategic Coach program, where I have learned so much. I'd also like to express my appreciation for my coaches, Colleen Bowler and Valentine Chavez-Gonzalez, for helping me through multiple business transitions and helping me develop the tools to balance family and business.

Of course, I could never have achieved anything without my amazing team. I take great pride in the fact I have surrounded myself with the best in the business!

I would be remiss if I left out my pastor, Charlie Couch, who helped save my marriage.

And, once again, I have to thank my family for inspiring this book and providing the motivation to try to be better every single day.

ABOUT THE AUTHOR

PATRICK CUMMINGS IS AN ENTREPRENEUR, BUSINESS coach, and wealth management advisor committed to helping others balance their lives for happier outcomes. He worked in the corporate world for twelve years before deciding, when his children were toddlers, to start his own business and gain control of his time. An active member of his community, Patrick lives in Washington State with his wife, Brooke.